WRITING FIGHT SCENES

Copyright © 2011-2015 Rayne Hall

All Rights Reserved

Cover Art and Design by Erica Syverson

Scimitar Press, St. Leonards

February 2015 Paperback Edition

WRITING FIGHT SCENES

Rayne Hall

CONTENTS

Introduction - 9

1. Gritty or Entertaining? -13

The gritty fight scene and the entertaining fight scene. Blending entertainment and grit. Which style for which genre? How much violence does a fight scene need? Blunders to avoid.

2. Location - 17

Use the setting to add entertainment, realism and suspense. Blunders to avoid.

3. Structure - 22

A blueprint for your scene in six parts: Suspense, Start, Action, Surprise, Climax, Aftermath.

4. Swords - 26

Three main types: thrusting, cleaving and slashing. Blunders to avoid.

5. Knives and Daggers - 30

Dagger or knife? Concealment. Connotations. Fighting techniques. Blunders to avoid.

6 Staffs, Spears and Polearms - 36

Thrusting and throwing spears. Poleaxes, billhooks, halberds. Blunders to avoid.

7. Clubs, Maces, Axes, Slings and Arrows - 40

Historical clubbing and cleaving weapons. Archery. Blunders to avoid.

8. Firearms - 45

Three main types: rifle, handgun, shotgun. Blunders to avoid.

9. Improvised Weapons – 48

What a resourceful character may use at a pinch, and why readers love it.

10. Magical Weapons and Warfare - 51

Inventing a plausible magical weapon. How to defeat a magician. Magical warfare. Blunders to avoid.

11. Unarmed Combat - 57

Hand-to-hand fighting. Two types: grappling and striking martial arts. Inventing a fantasy martial art. Who wins? Blunders to avoid.

12. Self-Defence - 63

Why readers love self-defence scenes. Self-defence for the skilled martial artists. Self-defence ideas the inexperienced fighter. Blunders to avoid.

13. Strength, Skill and Strategy - 69

How much strength, skill and strategy do fighters need, and where do they get them? Blunders to avoid.

14. Psychological Barriers - 74

Reluctance to fight. Reality shock for martial artists.' The 'freeze'.

15. Female Fighters – 77

Reader expectations. Physical and psychological differences. Skills and backstory. Inexperienced female fighters. Different fighting styles. Female curves of arousal. Women and weapons. Female soldiers. Clothing and armour. Blunders to avoid.

16. Male Fighters - 89

Characteristic male dialogue and body language. Skills. Men and their weapons. Male curves of arousal. Men against women. Blunders to avoid.

17. Animals and Weres - 95

How animals fight. Writing from an animal's point of view. Were-animals. Animals as weapons: dogs, horses, elephants. Fighting against an animal. Blunders to avoid.

18. Make the reader care - 103

Purpose and motivation. Raising the stakes. Emotion. Stacking the odds. Manipulate the reader's instincts. Blunders to avoid.

19. The Inside Experience - 110

Deep point of view. Using the senses: which sense in which part of the fight? Blunders to avoid.

20. Armour - 117

Historical and modern armour. Shields. Blunders to avoid.

21. Fight Situations - 122

Brawl. Duel. Ambush. Assassination. Riot.

22. Group vs Group, One vs Many - 128

Managing the point of view and reader sympathies. How to make a one-against-many fight plausible. Blunders to avoid.

23. Battles - 134

Plotting and structuring a battle scene. Blunders to avoid.

24. Siege Warfare - 139

Active and passive siege warfare. Blunders to avoid.

25. Nautical Fights - 143

Tips for pirate fights and naval battles. Destroy, plunder or capture? Boat or Ship? Blunders to avoid.

26. Genres - 149

Tips for romance, humour, fantasy, horror, thriller, mystery, historical literary, young adult and children's fiction.

27. Erotic Tension - 155

Hand-to-hand fighting. The erotic connotations of daggers. Male fantasies of female fighters. Post-fight horniness.

28. The Final Showdown - 160

The big fight between the hero and the villain at the end of the book. Blunders to avoid.

29. Pacing - 163

Tricks for fast pace. Word choices and sentence structures. When and how to slow the pace. Blunders to avoid.

30. Euphonics - 169

Subtle techniques for creating a mood of foreboding, fear, hard action, defeat or victory.

31. Sabre-Sharp Dialogue - 173

How to make it sound real. Witty zingers. Catchphrases. Blunders to avoid.

32. Background Music - 177

Tunes to put you in the mood.

33. Research - 179

Where to find out more.

34. Excerpts - 183

Two fight scenes by Rayne Hall

Dear Reader - 191

INTRODUCTION

This book will help you to write a fight scene which is entertaining as well as realistic, and leaves the reader breathless with excitement.

You may be clueless about fighting matters, as many authors are. The book will show you step-by-step how to write plausible fights and avoid blunders.

On the other hand, you may be a skilled martial artist, a military historian or a combat veteran. Then the book will guide you to turn your knowledge into vivid fiction.

I'll give you a six-part structure to use as blueprint for your scene, and reveal tricks how to combine fighting with dialogue, which senses to use when and how, and how to stir the reader's emotions. You'll decide how much violence your scene needs, what's the best location, how your heroine can get out of trouble with self-defence and how to adapt your writing style to the fast pace of the action. There will be sections on female fighters, male fighters, animals and weres, psychological obstacles, battles, duels, brawls, riots and final showdowns. For the requirements of your genre, there is even advice on how to build erotic tension in a fight scene, how magicians fight, how pirates capture ships and much more. You will learn about different types of weapons, how to use them in fiction, and how to avoid embarrassing blunders.

A few years ago, when I struggled with my fight scenes, I looked for guidance and found none. So I set about discovering for myself what makes a great fight scene. I studied famous fight scenes in classic literature and in modern thrillers, observed their structure and analysed their techniques.

Armed with these insights, I wrote fight scenes which enthralled the readers. Before long, other writers asked me to help me improve their fights. From there, it was a small step to teaching online classes in Writing Fight Scenes. All the time, I continued studying the subject and adding to my knowledge.

When I look back on my early fight scene attempts, I cringe – the mistakes are so glaring, the structure so awkward, the style so embarrassing. Now I know how to make a fight scenes work, and I want to share these techniques with you.

My expertise lies in the craft of fight scene writing, not in fighting. I'm a writer, not a warrior. A real fighter could easily beat the crap out of me. I could write a really good scene about it afterwards.

Although I've trained in several martial arts forms (mostly kickboxing, some self-defence, a little karate and aikido, even a spot of professional wrestling), I haven't won any match trophies or earned any black belts. My real-life fighting experiences include defending myself against a lecher in a rowing boat by hitting an oar over his head, and chasing away the neighbourhood bully with a garden spade.

When it comes to weapons, I know quite a bit about ancient arms and armour. I collect ancient arrowheads, and have flint-knapped my own set of stone age weaponry. I've practised archery (with considerable success), spear-throwing (so-so), and stone-slinging (abject failure).

As a belly dancer, I had an act where I balanced five blunted swords on different parts of my body. Although the weight of the swords led to hellish pain in my joints, audiences loved the show.

I've choreographed sword and staff fights for stage performances. While stage fights are very different from real fights, they have a lot in common with fight scenes in fiction.

The chapters give advice for different types of fights, weapons and genres, some of which will be relevant to your story and some which won't. Simply skip what you don't need.

This is a book about the craft of writing. It won't turn you into military historian or weapons expert, and it won't teach you how to fight.

While you don't need fighting experience to use this book, you need a basic understanding of the writing craft. If you're a beginner, I recommend you study a book on general fiction techniques first.

I'm using British English. If you're used to American English, some of the words and spellings may look odd, but I'm sure you'll understand me anyway.

When talking about characters, I'll use 'she' sometimes and 'he' at other times. With the exception of Chapters 15 and 16, almost everything I say applies regardless of gender.

Throughout the book, I'll suggest links to websites worth visiting for more information. I assume that their content is legal and correct, but I have no way of knowing, and accept no responsibility for them. Site owners change the content all the time, web pages get deleted and sites close down in the blink of an eye. If you find an inappropriate or dead link, let me know. You'll find my e-mail address at the end of this book.

I've viewed thousands of YouTube clips and selected those most useful for writers: martial arts displays, historical re-enactments, weapons demonstrations and self-defence advice. If you don't need them, just skip them.

The URLs are intended for the ebook edition where readers can simply click the links. They're less practical in the paperback, but readers have asked me to keep them anyway.

11

The guidelines in this book are intended as suggestions, not as rules. Every story is different; choose what suits yours.

I hope you'll enjoy my book and will apply the tricks to create fight scenes which are so entertaining, so realistic, so exciting that they stay in the reader's mind.

Rayne Hall

CHAPTER 1: GRITTY OR ENTERTAINING?

There are two types of fight scenes in fiction: entertaining ones, and gritty ones. Before you draft your fight scenes, decide to which group they belong.

THE GRITTY FIGHT SCENE

This type shows violence as it is: Nasty, brutal and quick. The typical gritty fight scene could be written in three words:

Slash. Gore. Dead.

In this type of scene, the actual fight is over quickly. The build-up to the fight is slow and suspenseful, and the Aftermath is prolonged. The fighters sustain terrible injuries, with spurting blood and welling gore. The Aftermath is horrid, with mutilated corpses, guts spilling from slashed bellies, and people dying in their own excrement.

The gritty fight scene invites the reader to feel revulsion and horror. Its purpose is to shock. Critics say that these fight scenes desensitise people to violence.

Watch an example

The duel scene from *Sanjuro* is perhaps the most famous gritty sword fight in film history. It's not on YouTube because of copyright reasons. Watch the movie if you get a chance, and note how quickly the actual fighting action is over.

THE ENTERTAINING FIGHT SCENE

This scene is heroic, spectacular, exciting, acrobatic, entertaining, theatrical, fun. It allows the protagonist to show honourable behaviour and display impressive skills.

The fighting Action is prolonged while the Aftermath is often non-existent.

Entertaining fight scenes can be unrealistic: The hero finishes off five attackers without breaking a sweat. There's little blood and no gore, and wounds are mere scratches. If there's any blood, it blooms like a red rose on a white shirt. The hero may get a slash on his cheek which will heal into a fetching scar, while the loser limps off with a couple of bruises and lives to fight another day. Death is rare. Even if someone dies, they finish as decorative corpses.

The entertaining fight scene uses the location creatively: fighters leap across gorges, slide down banisters, jump onto tables, somersault across motorbikes, swing from rafters. The Action involves jumping, spinning, whirling, twirling and acrobatic feats.

The entertaining fight scene invites the reader to feel admiration for the fighters' skill. Its purpose is to entertain. Critics say that these scenes fight scenes glorify violence.

Watch an example

This scene from *The Princes Bride* is one of the most popular fight scenes ever. Observe how the Action incorporates the location, how the fighters perform acrobatic feats, and how they manage to exchange verbal banter at the same time as sword blows.   **http://www.youtube.com/watch?v=8-66KBi_NM0**

BLENDING ENTERTAINMENT AND GRIT

Many entertaining fight scenes contain a touch of gritty realism, and many gritty fight scenes contain heroic elements.

You may model your fight scene on one of the two types, and temper it with elements from the other. For example, if you write romance, you may choose to make your fight scenes entertaining, with a healthy dose of realistic grit added. If you write a thriller, you may want to make your fight scenes gritty, but prolong them and give your hero the chance to show off his skill.

Watch an example

This scene from *Kill Bill 1* is essentially an entertaining fight scene (one against many, prolonged Action, skills display, acrobatic feats, creative use of the location, unrealistic outcome), while also containing strong gritty elements (brutality and a lot of spurting blood). **http://www.youtube.com/watch?v=a3aFv8IQb4s**

WHICH STYLE IS BETTER?

This depends on your personal taste. Think about the fight scenes you've read or watched, whether they were gritty or entertaining, and whether you enjoyed them. If the thought of brutal violence makes you sick, and if you can't stand the sight of blood, don't attempt to write a gritty scene.

It also depends on the genre. Some genres (e.g. horror, thriller) call for gritty fight scenes with or without entertaining elements. Others (e.g. children's novels) require entertaining fight scenes with or without grit. Fight scenes in romance novels are always more entertaining than gritty. Some sub-genres (e.g. paranormal romance) contain more gritty elements than others (e.g. Regency romance).

Read how other writers in your chosen genre and sub-genre have handled their fight scenes. If you're writing for a specific publisher or imprint, check how entertaining or gritty those fight scenes usually are, and model yours on them.

15

HOW MUCH VIOLENCE DOES YOUR FIGHT SCENE NEED?

If you're writing 'gritty': a lot. If you're writing 'entertaining': very little.

Do you want to create realism without violence? Insert a sentence about how the ground feels underfoot. This always adds a touch of realism to a fight scene.

Do you want to use realistic violence without grossing the reader out? Make the violence graphic, but keep it short. Most readers can stomach one or two sentences of graphic descriptions. The famous Greek epics *The Iliad* and *The Odyssey* by Homer used this technique 3,000 years ago, and it still works for modern authors.

Do you want to shock the readers without disgusting them? Describe a couple of gory details – the sound of blood dripping from the ceiling, the eyeball hanging down someone's cheek – but not more. Leave the rest implied.

BLUNDERS TO AVOID

* Implausible acrobatic feats in an otherwise realistic novel

* Loads of disgusting gore in a genre whose readers want gentle escapism

CHAPTER 2: LOCATION

Make your fight scene interesting by placing it in an unusual venue.

What's the weirdest place where your fight scene can happen? How about a sauna, a laundrette, a playground, a potter's workshop, a lady's boudoir, a cow shed, a minaret, a sculpture gallery, a stalactite cave, a theatre's prop storeroom, a sewage tunnel, a wine cellar or a morgue?

The location makes your fight scene memorable: an unusual setting lifts your fight scene above the common dark alleyways and barroom brawls. Select the quirkiest place that's still plausible.

ADD ENTERTAINMENT

The location can make your fight scene entertaining: What features are there that the fighters can jump on, leap across, climb up, swing from, duck under? What items can they topple or toss? The more creatively you use the space, the more entertaining the scene becomes.

In a long fight scene, the fight can move right across the terrain. This adds variety. Try to arrange it so the Climax of the fight happens in the most dangerous place – at the edge of the cliff, at the top of the tower, on the narrow crumbling wall.

The most popular location for entertaining fight scenes are stairs.

The fighters can stand on the steps, they can run or leap, they can stumble, fall or tumble, and maybe slide down the banister. They can also use the stairs to move from one location to another, which is useful in prolonged entertaining scenes. To make your fight scene stand out, make the stairs unusual in some way. Perhaps they've been freshly washed and are still slippery, or maybe they are so dilapidated that some boards are missing.

ADD REALISM

Location can also make your fight scene realistic. As soon as you mention what kind of ground the combatants are fighting on, the scene gains realistic flavour. what's the ground like: Persian rugs? Concrete? Lawn? Uneven planks of splintered wood? Hard, firm, soft, squishy, muddy, wet, slippery, wobbling, cluttered, sloping? I suggest mentioning the ground twice: once to show how it feels underfoot, and once to show how it affects the fight. Perhaps your heroine slips on the wet asphalt, or stumbles across the edge of a rug.

To keep your fight scene plausible, consider how large the space is. How much room do the combatants have to fight? How high is the ceiling? What obstacles restrict the space? For example: the hero is a warrior, used to swinging his sword in a high arc. Now he must fight indoors, where the ceiling is too low to raise the sword overhead. How will he cope? Spatial restrictions make the fight scene authentic, plausible and interesting.

Most staircases are too narrow for big sword swings, which can add interesting difficulties. In medieval castles, spiral staircases were almost always built so they favoured right-handed defenders. The person coming down had room to swing the sword-arm, while the person coming up had not. This makes an interesting challenge for the hero fighting his way up, or for a left-handed defender.

ADD SUSPENSE

How does a fighter become aware of the enemy's approach? You can use the setting to make this suspenseful.

Examples

* Although the point-of-view character sees nothing in the night-dark forest, he hears the cracking of breaking twigs.

* Fog shrouds the landscape, veiling the approach of the enemy army.

* While bathing at the edge of a clear lake, the heroine sees a second figure reflected in the water's surface.

* The hero is having a drink in a pub and spots the villain's arrival in the mirror above the bar.

* The evening sun is in the hero's back and throws long shadows. He sees his attacker's shadow just in time to spin around and deflect the knife attack.

To create additional Suspense immediately before the fight, describe some of the noises of the location: the croaking of a bird, the slamming of a door, the roar of a lorry on the nearby road.

SHOW THE LOCATION BEFORE THE FIGHT

During the fast action of the fight, there's no room for describing the setting. This can be confusing for the reader. To help the reader understand the location, show it in advance.

You can do this in the paragraphs preceding the fight, from the PoV's perspective. It's natural that someone who expects a fight checks out the location. The setting description before the fight can serve to create Suspense.

You can also do it in a previous scene. Perhaps the protagonist visits the place for a different purpose. This can create a delicious contrast.

Examples

* In one scene, the heroine descends the grand staircase in her ball gown, oozing feminine charm. In another scene, she leaps down the same stairs, dagger in hand.

* In one scene, the downtrodden maid scrubs the stairs and polishes the marble banister. In another, she slides down that banister, holding the mop handle as a pike before her.

* In one scene, the hero repairs a roof gutter and drainpipe. In another, he climbs up that drainpipe and swings from the roof gutter.

* In one scene, the botanist measures and studies the lianas in the jungle. In another, he uses them to swing across the river.

If the plot doesn't permit showing the exact location before the fight begins, try to show a similar place. For example, if the fight scene takes place in a previously undiscovered ancient catacomb, show the protagonist in another catacomb earlier in the book.

Watch examples

Observe how the location and its features are used in these famous fight scenes:

http://www.youtube.com/watch?v=l0JYNznbL0Q (*First Strike*)

http://www.youtube.com/watch?v=8-66KBi_NM0 (*The Princess Bride*)

http://www.youtube.com/watch?v=JxWA4GPtM6Q (*Robin of Sherwood*) http://www.youtube.com/watch?v=a3aFv8IQb4s (*Kill Bill 1*)

http://www.youtube.com/watch?v=uGzdusxI5XA (*Snatch*)

http://www.youtube.com/watch?v=PfVYaK7VFOY (*Dynasty*)

BLUNDERS TO AVOID

* Generic setting... as if the fight took place in 'white space'

* Actions for which there isn't enough room, e.g. swinging swords overhead in indoors scenes

CHAPTER 3: STRUCTURING YOUR FIGHT SCENE

Now it's time to plot your fight. Here's a blueprint for a scene structured in six parts. Feel free to use it as is, or to adapt it to suit your vision.

1. SUSPENSE

This is before the actual fight starts. Your PoV lies in ambush, or waits for the officer's command to storm the fortress. He checks his equipment one last time, or counts the twenty paces for the duel. (Don't include how he gets up in the morning, eats breakfast, walks his dog and rides to the duelling site). The pace is slow, the Suspense is high.

In this section, you can provide the reader with information about terrain, numbers, equipment, weapons, weather. The Suspense section may also contain dialogue as the opponents taunt each other, hurl accusations, or make one final effort to avoid the slaughter. Use Suspense techniques (e.g. describe background noises, or employ the 'ticking clock' effect).

2. START

The fighters get into fighting stance – whatever fighting stance is appropriate for the weapon. In unarmed combat, the typical stance looks like this: knees slightly bent, one leg further forward than the other, the body turned diagonally, the abdominal muscles tightened but not pulled in, the hands balled as fists near the face. In most kinds of armed fighting, the one who gets the first strike has the greatest advantage, so each will try to be the first.

During this section, the fighters assess their opponents' skill. The moves in this section need to be specific and technically correct. In an entertaining fight scene, this section may contain dialogue.

3. ACTION

In a 'gritty' scene, this part is over quickly. In an 'entertaining' scene, this part is prolonged. Blow-by-blow accounts of every movement are unnecessary in this section. Instead, focus on the overall direction of the fight *(Sheena parried the blows with all her strength, but the enemy drove her closer and closer to the abyss.)* Use the location creatively, especially if this is an entertaining fight scene (this is where the fighters duck, climb, jump, swing and leap). Mention the sounds of the weapons *(Steel clanked against steel).* There is probably no dialogue.

4. SURPRISE

Something happens that is outside the fighters' control and that affects the fighting. It may have to do with the setting, with the weapons, or with other people: A sudden downpour turns the ground into slippery mud. The staircase collapses. The building bursts into flames. The relief force arrives. An innocent bystander stumbles into the fight. The hero has his weapon knocked from his hand and has to continue the fight empty-handed. A bullet smashes the single light bulb and the place goes dark. In professional wrestling, this is called 'outside interference'.

The Surprise event should change the way the fight scene goes, but it should never end the fight. The Surprise event adds interest and excitement to the entertaining fight scene. Gritty scenes seldom have this section.

5. CLIMAX

This is the most exciting part of the scene, and the fighting is at its most intense. Both fighters are tired, perhaps wounded. Your PoV may be close to giving up, but then she remembers her purpose, and the passion revives her. The Climax often moves to the location's weirdest, most dangerous spot: a narrow swinging rope-bridge, a trapeze high up in a circus tent, a roof-edge, a sinking ship.

Describe the final moves of the fight in technically correct detail, especially the decisive stroke.

6. AFTERMATH

The fight is over. The PoV takes stock, counts his bruises, feels the pain, bandages his wounds, discusses the result with other survivors, and comes to terms with the emotional effects such as his best buddy lying dead. Use the senses of sight and smell. The PoV may experience nausea, shaking or tearfulness, or he may get sexually horny; these are the after-effects of the adrenaline and hormones released into his bloodstream earlier.

In an entertaining scene, this section may be short, but for the sake of realism, I recommend writing at least two sentences about the Aftermath. In gritty scenes, this section is often the longest part, showing grisly details and harrowing emotions.

HOW LONG IS YOUR FIGHT SCENE?

Fight scenes can be any length between 25 and 2,500 words.

If it's 25 words, it's probably not a proper scene, rather part of a bigger scene. If it's 2,500 words, it needs to be remarkably good to hold the reader's interest. If it's longer, it may be better to treat it as a series of several short scenes.

Fight scenes in historical, adventure and fantasy fiction are often around 700-1000 words long. In romance, they tend to be shorter. If you're new to fight scene writing, I recommend keeping the scene short-ish – say, 400-700 words. But don't be tempted to spend most of these words on the Suspense section, or the reader may feel you've cheated them of the Action experience.

If a novel contains several fight scenes, then the last one (the climactic showdown between hero and villain) is probably the longest.

EXAMPLES FROM THE MOVIES

Here are some famous fight examples worth studying. When watching these, see if you can identify the six parts (not every scene has all six). Observe how the Suspense part is constructed.

http://www.youtube.com/watch?v=hf4IoxEUmHM&featu re=related (*Troy*)

http://www.youtube.com/watch?v-8-66KBi_NM0(*The Princess Bride)*

Also try watch the duel scene from *Rob Roy* which is a perfect example. Because of copyright reasons, it's been removed from YouTube, but it's worth studying.

BLUNDERS TO AVOID

* Starting the scene too early. (Hero gets out of bed, dresses, brushes his teeth, saddles his horse, rides to the site, dismounts...)

* Rushing the Climax. (Not giving it as much space as it deserves)

* Technical blow-by-blow account of the whole fight

CHAPTER 4: SWORDS

The sword is the most popular weapon in historical and fantasy fiction, where it lends itself to entertaining show-offs as well as to gritty butchery, and readers adore the mystique of the sword. However, if you don't understand swords, it's easy to commit blunders which make the scene ridiculous.

To bluff your way through a sword fight scene, simply pick one of these three sword types:

THE THRUSTING SWORD

Type of fight scene: entertaining, duels, non-lethal fights, non-gory deaths, swashbuckling adventure

Mostly used in: Europe, including Renaissance and Regency periods

Typical user: slim, male or female, good aerobic fitness

Main action: thrust, pierce, stab

Main motion: horizontal with the tip forward

Shape: straight, often thin, may be lightweight

Typical injury: seeping blood, blood stains spreading.

Strategy for lethal fight: target gaps in the armour, pierce a vital organ

Disadvantage: cannot slice through bone or armour

Examples: gladius, rapier, foil, epée

Watch in action:

http://www.youtube.com/watch?v=nITldg2dOVk

THE CLEAVING SWORD

Type of fight scene: gritty, brutal, battles, cutting through armour

Typical user: tall brawny male with broad shoulders and bulging biceps

Mostly used in: Medieval Europe

Main action: cleave, hack, chop, cut, split

Main motion: downwards

Shape: broad, straight, heavy, solid, sometimes huge, sometimes needs to be held in both hands, both edges sharpened.

Typical injury: severed large limbs

Strategy for lethal fight: hack off a leg, then decapitate; or split the skull

Disadvantages: Too big to carry concealed, too heavy to carry in daily life, too slow to draw for spontaneous action

Examples: Medieval greatsword, Scottish claymore (the older type), machete, falchion

Watch in action:

http://www.youtube.com/watch?v=_hfLZozBVpM

THE SLASHING SWORD

Type of fight scene: gritty or entertaining, executions, cavalry charge, on board a ship

Mostly used in: Asia, Middle East

Typical user: male (female is plausible), any body shape, Arab, Asian, mounted warrior, cavalryman, sailor, pirate

Main action: slash, cut, slice

Main motion: fluid, continuous, curving, e.g. figure-eight

Shape: curved, often slender, extremely sharp on the outer edge

Typical injury: severed limbs, lots of spurting blood

Disadvantages: unable to cut through hard objects (e.g. metal armour)

Strategy for lethal fight: first disable opponent's sword hand (e.g. cut off hand or slice into tendons inside the elbow), then slash a vital artery (e.g. on thigh or neck)

Examples: scimitar, sabre, saif, shamshir, cutlass, katana

Watch in action:

**http://www.youtube.com/watch?v=qapwAIemccg,
http://www.youtube.com/watch?v=R-qpedUbxBc**

MULTI-PURPOSE SWORDS AND MIXED-SWORD MATCHES

In reality, the lines are often blurred: Some stabbing swords can also slash, some slashing swords can cleave, and some cleaving swords can deliver a thrust. But if you're a novice to swords, play it safe and stick to one main function. That's the safest way to avoid laughable mistakes.

Most swords have a sharp tip which can deliver a final thrust to kill an enemy who's already down.

Opponents with different types of swords can make fight scenes exciting – but you need to be a swordcraft expert to pull this off. If you don't have that level of knowledge, keep it simple and stick to one type.

BLUNDERS TO AVOID

* Inventing a fancy weapon for the hero... as if a gimmicky-shaped sword stood a chance against a blade of tried-and-tested standard design

* Weapons from the wrong period... as if an ancient Greek would use a medieval greatsword, or a Norman knight a 19th century cavalry sabre

* Generic sword which can hack, slash, cleave, stab, slice, pierce, thrust, cut through armour, split bricks and whirl through the air... as if a single sword could do everything

* Weapons performing tasks they can't do... as if an epée sword could split skulls, or a scimitar could fly through the air and nail a body to a wall

* Protagonists fighting with swords for which they don't have the strength or build... as if a dainty girl could run across the battlefield swinging a two-handed greatsword

* The hero carrying his huge sword with him at all times, immediately ready to draw

* Drawing a big sword from a sheath on the back (a physical impossibility)

CHAPTER 5: KNIVES AND DAGGERS

For historical fiction, a dagger is the ideal weapon: plausible in many scenarios, and loaded with emotional connotations. Yet, it's under-used, because few writers grasp the dagger's fiction potential.

Many authors write sword fight scenes where a dagger fight would be more plausible. Swords are large and heavy, cumbersome to carry, slow to draw, and almost impossible to conceal. In many situations, it's unlikely that a protagonist happens to carry a sword with him. By contrast, daggers are small, lightweight, quick to draw, and easy to conceal – perfect for quick responses, spontaneous action, brawls, suicide bids, self-defence and assassination.

While only people of wealth and rank can afford a sword, owning a dagger is feasible for all but the poorest. Wielding a dagger requires only moderate strength, which makes it a plausible weapon for a lady. Even an injured person may be able to summon the strength for a final defence with a dagger.

For almost every scene, the dagger is a better choice than the sword (the exceptions are horseback fights and battle scenes).

Here is a series of clips demonstrating how to fight with different types of historical knives and daggers:

http://www.youtube.com/watch?v=Ys6zON34qGg&feature=related

http://www.youtube.com/watch?v=fUoeZW4cwUE&feature=related

http://www.youtube.com/watch?v=ryQST1FST_4&feature=related

DAGGER OR KNIFE?

There's no clear distinction between knives and daggers; sometimes both words are used for the same weapon. In general, the dagger is designed mostly for thrusting and the knife mostly for cutting (slashing). A knife usually has only one sharp edge, while most daggers have two.

CONCEALMENT

The concealment offers exciting fictional opportunities. Typically, a dagger is carried in a leather sheath on the belt, easily concealed under a cloak if required. For secrecy, it can also be hidden in a boot or in a bodice. Indeed, during the Renaissance, it was quite common for women to carry a dagger between their breasts (the sheath was sewn into the bodice). A dagger can also be concealed in the back of the bodice or in a hair ornament. The heroine, preparing to fight off a lecherous advance or to assassinate an enemy, can pretend to twist her necklace anxiously, or to fidget with her hair, and quickly draw the blade. Bodice daggers have hilts without cross guards.

Here's a picture of a bodice dagger:

http://www.knifemaker.co.uk/Gallery/Gallery%20Images/Art%20Images/Bodice/bodice.html

CONNOTATIONS

Besides its many practical uses, the dagger carries a lot of emotional and erotic symbolism.

To stab someone with a dagger, the fighter has to get close, which makes it one of the most intimate weapons. When the dagger penetrates the flesh, the hand almost touches the victim. This is very different from a bullet or arrow, which can be shot from a great distance.

The closeness creates an intensely personal connection between attacker and victim. Daggers (and knives of all kinds) are often used in fights where emotions are running high: gang warfare, hate crime, vengeance.

The shape of the weapon and the fact that it's typically worn on the belt make it a symbol of male virility. In many cultures and periods, men demonstrated their manhood by displaying ornate daggers at the front of their hips, the bigger, the better.

Sometimes the hilt rather than the blade was exaggerated: Many daggers from 1200 to 1800, especially in England and Scotland, had huge, stiff, upwards-pointing wooden hilts with balls on either side. They were unblushingly called 'bollocks daggers' (or 'ballock daggers').

FIGHTING TECHNIQUES

Daggers are stabbing weapons with sharp points, usually with long, thin blades. When describing a stab wound, show blood spreading or oozing. The aim in a fight is to stab a vital organ such as kidneys, liver, bowel, stomach, heart. Stabbing directly at the chest seldom works, because the blade may glance off the ribs.

If the fighter has dagger experience or anatomical knowledge, she will position the dagger below the ribcage and drive it upwards (through the diaphragm into the lungs). This is lethal and works from the front or from behind. If she knows her anatomy well (e.g. if she's a professional assassin), and if the dagger is long enough, she can aim for piercing the heart, which leads to a quicker death. Trained assassins know additional spots where a stab is lethal, e.g. under the armpit or under the chin.

If your heroine doesn't know anatomy, repeated thrusts at the abdomen will eventually pierce one of the vital organs.

Many daggers are designed for slashing as well as stabbing. These have one or two sharp edges.

When describing a slash wound, show a lot of blood, streaming or even spurting. The aim in a fight with this type of dagger is either to slash the opponent's throat, or to disable him by cutting tendons, muscles or ligaments (perhaps followed with a deadly stab). Cutting the muscles in the weapon-wielding arm is the most effective technique. Slashing the inside of the wrist or the back of the knee also ends the fight. Fights with slashing daggers are very bloody. The point-of-view character's hand may grow slick with blood, and her grip on the weapon may become less firm.

If you're aiming for a sanitised, gore-free version of a dagger fight, you may want to stick to pure stabbing daggers.

Assassination

For an assassination scene, give your assassin stealth and knowledge of human anatomy. An assassin will plan in advance how to kill the victim, and carry out the killing with calm efficiency. It will be with a single stroke, probably a determined thrust from below the ribs.

Self-defence

If your PoV uses a knife to defend herself, she needs to disable the attacker's hand which holds his weapon, for example, with a slash at the inside of the elbow or wrist. The back of the knee will also incapacitate him. If it's a stabbing dagger, she needs to thrust rapidly many times, wherever she can hit. She won't have time to choose a suitable target area, and her attacker won't hold still while she positions the dagger. If the blade is too short to inflict serious damage, she can make up for this by stabbing so fast and so many times that the pain and blood-loss disable the attacker.

Vengeance and hatred

An attacker who is motivated by intense feelings, such as rancour or outrage, will stab the victim repeatedly, and keep stabbing, perhaps even after the victim is already dead. If the motive is long-held hatred, the attacker may stab or slash the victim's face, disfiguring it.

Contemporary street fights and gang warfare often involve knives, and they get passionate and bloody.

Duels

If both fighters are armed with daggers, the fight may include wrestling-type moves as each tries to restrict the other's weapon hand.

They will also try to disable each other's weapon arm, for example by slashing the inside of the elbow. Such fights are often fuelled by emotions, intense, irrational, very bloody, and fatal.

You can watch a demonstration of dagger fighting with wrestling moves here:

http://www.youtube.com/watch?v=z143thJWRBQ

Sword and dagger in combination

If a fighter expects a fight, e.g. in a battle, he may use both sword and dagger. He fights with the sword in his right hand and the dagger in his left. This was common during the Renaissance. Many medieval knights also carried daggers in addition to their swords or maces.

You can watch a sword and dagger demonstration here:
http://www.youtube.com/watch?v=IsR-C_P98r0

BLUNDERS TO AVOID

* Stabbing straight at the chest and hitting the heart (the ribs will deflect the blade).

* Hero uses stabbing dagger to slice his bread.

* Normal dagger used as a throwing dagger.

CHAPTER 6: STAFFS, SPEARS AND POLEARMS

This type of weapon can add authenticity to historical fiction, and allow the hero to display great skill in an entertaining scene.

STAFFS

The staff was an important weapon in many periods and many cultures, because it is inexpensive and – in the hands of a skilled fighter – deadly. In fiction, it is particularly useful for entertaining fight scenes, or for spontaneous fights. A fighter who is skilled with a staff can grab a broomstick or a garden hoe and use it as a staff.

The staff is a useful weapon for the petite heroine: it's much lighter than a sword, and it's long enough to keep a bigger, stronger attacker at a distance, so he can't tackle or grapple.

Watch in action

http://www.youtube.com/watch?v=fMe0tBBOgCs&feature=related (choreographed kung fu staff fight)

SPEARS

In most periods, spears were the most common weapon for warfare. Spears are cheaper than swords, which makes them suitable for equipping large armies, and affordable for commoners who had to provide their own arms. Spears can be tipped with metal (bronze or iron), with stone (knapped flint), with anything else at hand (bone, glass shards), or, at a pinch, simply have one end sharpened to a point. By equipping your common soldiers with spears, you can add realism to your battle scene.

There are two kinds of spears:

The throwing spear

At the start of the battle, the army throws lots of spears at the enemy to do as much damage as possible before closing in (example: the pilum used by the Roman army). Each soldier may carry several throwing spears. In many cultures, a device (the 'atlatl') is used for loading the spear on the shoulder and catapulting it forward, increasing its throwing power. The atlatl is a great equaliser, allowing women to hurl a spear with as much strength as a man. Once a spear is thrown, it cannot be used again – except by the enemy who might hurl it right back! Some spears are designed so their tips break on impact to prevent re-use. Throwing spears are fairly lightweight. The throwing spear is sometimes called 'javelin'.

The thrusting spear

This is often the main weapon of peasants pressed into military service, in which case it may be a converted farm implement. Among professional soldiers with military-issued equipment, the spears are often very long, and form an impenetrable barrier. Sometimes a spear-armed army awaits the enemy in this formation: The first row of soldiers kneels with spears low in hand. The second row, close behind them, kneels with spears at hip height. The third row stands with spears at waist height. The fourth holds the spears at shoulder height, and the fifth holds them above. Thus, the attacking army faced a wall of several dense rows of spears! The ancient Macedonians and the Renaissance pikemen used this kind of formation with great success. The thrusting spear is sometimes called a 'lance'. If it's very long, it's called a 'pike'.

Warriors carry a shield to protect themselves against spear throws and thrusts. They may carry a spear in the right and a shield in the left.

Watch spears in action

http://www.youtube.com/watch?v=bpLtXIlkyYA (battle scene from *Troy* using a variety of weapons)

http://www.youtube.com/watch?v=xGiuKyHkwmw (spear throwing with atlatl)

http://www.youtube.com/watch?v=8kQwMbJpBTs (Macedonian pikes)

http://youtu.be/6p93xUp9GrQ (spear fighting technique)

POLEARMS

Polearms are thrusting spears with cleverly designed, large heads which can stab, cut, hook, twist, cleave, push or pull. They can be used as lances or as staffs, as well as for their specialist function, which makes them versatile weapons in medieval warfare. Although they serve best at a distance (preventing a sword-armed fighter from getting close), by holding them differently the fighter can use them close up as well. Some are even designed to prise open plate armour. Fiction writers rarely use them, but polearms can add authenticity to a medieval fight scene.

Here are three major types:

Poleaxe

This is a spear with a tip for thrusting combined with an axe-blade for cleaving.

Billhook

This was originally an agricultural tool, a hook-shaped blade for clearing brush. Adapted as a weapon, the billhook has a long handle, a long sharp spike as a tip, and a pronounced hook/blade which serves to pull and cut the enemy's legs and ankles.

Halberd

Originally, the halberd's head was a rectangular blade sharpened to a tip. Over the centuries, it was refined so it had an axe like blade on one side and a hook on the other, and developed especially to repel horses and to stop swordsmen getting close. Later, it became a ceremonial weapon, sometimes worn by guardsmen on parade.

Watch polearms in action

http://www.youtube.com/watch?v=XJuNgXUi-Bk
(polearm technique)

http://www.youtube.com/watch?v=OF0JpDiW33c&NR=1
(billhook demonstration at the end).

BLUNDERS TO AVOID

* Medieval battles in which every soldier has a sword and nobody fights with spears and polearms

* Soldiers carrying polearms and not using them

CHAPTER 7: CLUBS, MACES, AXES, SLINGS AND ARROWS

This chapter explores more weapons which can enrich historical novels.

CLUBS AND MACES

Wooden clubs were probably the earliest weapons, sometimes with spikes added to the head. Maces are refined versions of clubs, usually made from steel, and flanged or spiked. They are formidable weapons, perfect for smashing plate armour and for crushing skulls.

To use the club or mace, the fighter needs to get close to the opponent – not easy if that guy has a polearm or a long-handled battle axe. When using a mace on horseback, the rider uses a continuous swinging motion and leans to the side to which he is hitting. If the story is set in a period where horses were shorter than they are today, he doesn't have to lean far.

Type of fight scene: gritty, historical fiction, fantasy fiction, smashing armour

Typical user: brawny male with broad shoulders and bulging biceps

Mostly used in: historical fiction – Stone Age to Middle Ages

Main action: smash, crush, bludgeon, batter

Main motion: downwards

Typical injury: crushed bones, crushed skull

Strategy for lethal fight: crush skull

Disadvantages: heavy, need to get close to the opponent

Watch a mace in action

http://www.youtube.com/watch?v=-S87kkS5m5Y

BATTLE AXES

A peasant or lumberjack can use a common axe as a weapon. Special battle axes are bigger and heavier, often with longer handles, and they are formidable weapons.

An axe delivers a huge amount of force to a small area of strong, very sharp metal. It is a weapon for attack rather than defence, and good at cleaving through armour. It can break enemy shields and kill a charging horse. Since they require intense training, the users are mostly highly skilled elite soldiers, often aristocrats, e.g. the Saxon *huscarls*.

Type of fight scene: gritty, brutal, battles, attack, historical fiction, fantasy fiction, cutting through armour

Typical user: tall brawny male with broad shoulders and bulging biceps, courageous, elite soldier, Viking, Saxon

Mostly used in: European Dark Ages to Middle Ages

Main action: cleave, hack, chop, cut, split

Main motion: downwards

Typical injury: severed large limbs, split skulls, cleaved torsos

Strategy for lethal fight: severe the arm which holds the sword or the shield, or cleave torso from top to bottom, or cut off a leg then split the skull

Disadvantages: big and heavy

Watch battle axes in action

Here are three connected videos about Viking and Saxon warriors with axes:

http://www.youtube.com/watch?v=zhRCNLMzUMY&feature=related

http://www.youtube.com/watch?v=EYrOI-3bDKY&feature=related

http://www.youtube.com/watch?v=yaG_OO1RYE8&feature=related

BOWS AND ARROWS

Bows and arrows existed in almost all historical periods, although the technology and the shape of the bow varied.

They are weapons for mass use. At the beginning of a battle, hundreds of arrows are shot at the enemy to inflict as much damage as possible from a distance. In the middle of the battle and for close combat, they're useless. In the medieval period, archery frequently determined the outcome of the battle.

Arrows are also great for defence against a besieging force. Castles were designed for the use of bows and arrows, with very narrow windows called 'archer slits'. The top of the outer walls were designed so archers could shoot while remaining under cover.

Arrows are relatively cheap and quick to produce. The tips can be metal or sharpened stone (e.g. flint or obsidian), sharpened wood, bone, glass splinters etc. The wooden shaft needs to be straight. Pieces of feather at the end help the arrow fly better, but knowing which part of the feather to attach how and where is much-treasured knowledge.

Good bows, on the other hand, are difficult and time-consuming to produce, which makes them expensive, treasured possessions.

Learning the basics of archery is quick. In an emergency, your characters can learn in an afternoon how to shoot with reasonable accuracy. However, to be really good at it takes years of practice. The most important skill in a battle situation is being able to shoot many arrows in quick succession. Highly skilled archers were valued. Even when victorious besiegers put all inhabitants of a castle to death, they often spared the archers to add them to their own armies.

Some armies had mounted archers, skilled at shooting from horseback.

Many mythological heroes (Robin Hood, Wilhelm Tell, Karl Stuempner, Odysseus) performed archery feats.

When writing about archery, avoid the phrase 'to fire'. The correct term is 'to shoot'.

Watch bows and arrows in action

http://www.youtube.com/watch?v=HagCuGXJgUs
(Demonstration of medieval longbow and crossbow)

http://www.youtube.com/watch?v=uTWb_4u7J74
(Demonstration of ancient Roman archery)

http://youtu.be/BEG-ly9tQGk (historical archery technique for shooting in motion)

STONE SLINGS

Stone slings are the cheapest weapon to make. All it takes is a piece of leather and some string. Ammunition is simply pebbles lying around. It doesn't require great physical strength. However, it takes weeks of practice to achieve reasonable accuracy.

This makes it a suitable weapon for low-tech historical periods, and for people of all ages and body shapes (including children) who can't afford costly weapons but who have the time and opportunity to practice – for example, shepherd boys (like young David in the Bible).

Different cultures have different techniques for holding and releasing, none of which includes the continuous frantic whirling around and around beloved by movie-makers. This lessens the accuracy and increases the force only marginally. Many experts rotate the swing maybe once or twice, or not at all.

Here's one basic technique: The slinger hooks the end of the sling over her fingers, and holds the hand above the shoulder, so the sling's bag with the stone in it hangs down behind her shoulder. Then she flings it straight forward.

BLUNDERS TO AVOID

* Presenting an axeman as an unskilled brute who chops blindly.

* Battles where the archers shoot when the sword fighters are already engaged in close fighting

* Swinging a stone sling wildly around and around before releasing the stone

CHAPTER 8: FIREARMS

Real gunfights are over within seconds. This makes firearms more suitable for gritty than entertaining fight scenes.

THREE TYPES OF GUNS

Choose between these three main types of firearms.

The rifle

This is accurate and powerful, but difficult to conceal and relatively slow to use. The rifle is plausible in scenes where the fighter is prepared and ready to shoot (e.g. on a hunting trip, or defending their home against approaching marauders, or a professional sniper).

The handgun

This is easy to conceal and fast to draw, but not as accurate as the rifle and may not have much power (the bullet may pass right through the flesh and the person may keep running). The handgun is plausible in spontaneous fights, for law enforcement officers (or bad guys) who are always ready to shoot, and for unexpected self-defence situations.

The shotgun

This fires several pellets at once. It is useful for hitting small, fast-moving targets. Although its 'spread' is not as wide as some people imagine, it may endanger bystanders and can be problematic in hostage situations. Shotguns have an 'unheroic' image, and many readers don't like it if the hero uses one.

WRITING REALISTIC GUNFIGHTS

Of course, this is a simplistic breakdown, and if you're writing gunfights, it's worth researching the gun type of your choice.

To avoid blunders, make sure the chosen type of gun was available in the chosen period. While it's plausible that a fighter uses a twenty-year old gun, it's not plausible that he uses a gun which gets invented twenty years later. Bear in mind that historical firearms were far less accurate than modern ones.

Don't assume that people in other countries carry guns. American writers often get this wrong when they write about a Scottish heroine pulling a gun from her handbag or an English beat police officer engaging in a fire-fight with a criminal. Of course, a crime lord can obtain a gun anywhere in the world, but your law-abiding hero won't. The difference can be difficult to grasp for a writer who lives in a US state where licences to carry are available, but if you ignore this, your fight scene becomes implausible.

HITTING THE TARGET

Accuracy can only be achieved with practice. If your heroine fells the villain with a gunshot, this is only believable if she has had firearms training. Inexperienced shooters who pick up a gun for the first time and immediately hit their target are implausible.

If the plot requires hitting the target, then it's best if you mention beforehand that the shooter is a member of a gun club or trains at a shooting range.

Most shooters achieve far less accuracy in a real fight than while practising at the shooting range. This is because the adrenaline rush in the bloodstream makes a grip on the weapon slightly unsteady. It's possible that your hero, who hit the bullseye every time during the practice session, misses the target in a real fight, even if it's the same gun and the same distance.

Hitting a moving target is extremely difficult, and plausible only if the shooter is remarkably skilled.

For interesting plot complications, you can use 'ricochet': the bullet hits the wall instead of the opponent, bounces off, and hits someone else. Professionals know about the dangers of ricochet, and avoid shooting indoors or towards a wall – but in fiction, we can create situations where this cannot be avoided.

BLUNDERS TO AVOID

* Implausible feats of accuracy (especially with moving targets)

* Inexperienced person picks up a gun for the first time and immediately hits the distant target... as if accuracy didn't require practice

* Using a type of gun which was not invented yet in that period... as if a gunslinger in the Wild West could get hold of a Jericho 941 semi-automatic from Israel

* Weapons performing tasks they can't do... as if a small-calibre pistol could stop a running target at a thousand feet

* Police officers and law-abiding civilians carrying guns in countries where this is prohibited

CHAPTER 9: IMPROVISED WEAPONS

Readers love resourceful characters, and improvised weapons show resourcefulness.

Since women, when threatened, reflexively grab something to use as a weapon (men seldom do), you can delight the reader with your heroine's resourcefulness, and at the same time keep the scene psychologically plausible.

If your heroine defends herself with a garden hose, a toilet brush or a curling iron, the readers will root for her and enjoy the fight. This works especially well in 'entertaining' fight scenes, although you can also adapt it for 'gritty' scenes.

What items are within reach? If the attack happens while she's sitting at a desk, she may grab a letter opener – perfect for stabbing – or a paperweight (which can lend force to her boxing punch, or can be slammed on his head or thrown at him).

If she gets attacked while walking out of doors, she may have something useful in her bag or in her pockets:

* A pen is useful for stabbing, especially if thrusts it repeatedly at vulnerable body parts such as throat and eyes.

* A pointed key can inflict damage if held so the sharp tip pokes out between the fingers of a balled fist.

* Cologne spray spritzed into the attacker's eyes can blind him for a moment.

* A jogger can squeeze her water bottle into his eyes to gain a precious second or two.

* A small heavy object such as a pretty stone she picked up on the beach can lend power to her punches.

However, she won't have time to dig to the bottom of her bag in search of a useful item. It needs to be something she holds in her hand already, or can grab instantly.

The bag itself can be a useful tool, especially if it's heavy. Your heroine can grip it by the handle and swing it at the attacker, or slam it down on his head.

You can make the scene feel even more realistic by showing that your heroine is skilled at using this item in a non-fight situation. Consider the tools she uses in her job or her pastimes:

* The passionate knitter stabs her attacker with her knitting needles.

* The amateur gardener hits her assailant with the hose pipe, stabs him with secateurs, or hits a spade over his head.

* The cook slams the cast iron frying pan on his head.

* The hair stylist hits back with a wire brush, spritzes him with hairspray or a burns him with a hot curling iron

* The librarian hurls a heavy tome.

* The archaeologist applies her sharp pointed trowel.

* The cleaner hits with the mop, sloshes soapy water into his face, or sprays his eyes with antiseptic.

* The doctor whips him with her stethoscope or thrusts a scalpel into his flesh.

* The glamour model stabs him with a stiletto heel.

* The rower slams an oar over his head.

* The belly dancer clanks her finger cymbals at his ears so loudly that his eardrums burst.

* The jeweller stabs him with the pin of a brooch.

* The cashier throws a handful of coins into his face or bashes him under the ear with an unopened roll of pennies.

BLUNDERS TO AVOID

* The attacker stands still while the heroine rummages through her handbag in search of a weapon

* Before the attack, the heroine holds something in her hand, but during the attack, the item is forgotten

CHAPTER 10: MAGICAL WEAPONS AND WARFARE

The content of this chapter overlaps with a section in the book Writing About Magic.

When writing paranormal and fantasy fiction, we writers can invent fantastic weapons. However, these weapons need to be interesting so they enrich the story, and believable so the readers can suspend their disbelief.

A weapon which can kill anyone, any time, is implausible and boring.

Here are some ideas how to create a magic weapon, inspired by real magic traditions from different cultures. Your weapon probably includes some, but not all, of these ideas. Have fun!

MATERIAL, SIZE AND SHAPE

* The weapon is made from a solid, natural material: stone, wood, or bone. The bone could be from a ritually sacrificed animal, from a human ancestor, from a hero or saint, or from a slain enemy.

* It may contain a crystal, or a precious or semi-precious stone, because these are good at storing and intensifying magical energy.

* It has an elongated shape, like a wand or a staff. Indeed, it may be disguised as an everyday elongated object, such as a pen or a walking stick. The magician points it at the target, similar to aiming a gun.

* The weapon can be of any size, from a tiny jewellery pendant to a tree trunk. Small items have the advantage that the magicians can carry them on their body or hide them in their garments. Large items may be stationary and everyone knows of their existence and location.

* There is probably a religious connection. For example, the weapon may be sacred to a goddess, blessed in a temple, manufactured by monks, invented by a god, given to the hero by a goddess.

* It is probably old, perhaps inherited through generations.

* It can only be given – for example, in gratitude by the craftsman who made it, or granted by a priestess on her deathbed. It can't be bought with money.

* The manufacture of the weapon involved a ritual and a sacrifice. This may have been a human sacrifice. The weapon may have been dipped into the sacrificial victim's blood.

HOW IT WORKS

* Most magic works through the user's mind. To activate the weapon, the magician needs to concentrate, perhaps think a certain sequence of thoughts. The use of a magical weapon is never purely physical (such as pulling the trigger on a gun). It's the mental effort that counts. This can create interesting situations when the magician needs to concentrate to use the weapon, but can't concentrate in the heat of the battle.

* The damage inflicted by a magical weapon may be invisible. It may kill without leaving visible wounds, baffling the healers or coroners.

* Magical weapons may act slowly. A person may get hit by a magical weapon and not realise it until hours or days later, by which time it's too late to seek help.

* The weapon may affect the target's mind rather than the body. For example, it may rob that person of the will to live, or of the courage to fight.

* Many magical weapons work on one of the elements (earth, air, fire, water). For example, the weapon may kill by shaking the earth on which the target stands, or by heating the air the target breathes.

* The weapon can hit hidden targets. Its energy can move through or around obstacles.

* The user needs training to wield the weapon. This probably involves training in magic (power raising, mental focus, directing energy), as well as training in the use of the specific weapon. In the hands of an untrained person, the weapon may be ineffective, or may kill the user.

CHARGING AND CLEANSING

* Before use, the weapon needs to be magically fuelled (the usual term for this is 'charged'). This may be done in a certain place (at a spring, in a temple, at a crossroads) or by a certain person (a senior magician, a crone, a priestess). The charge involves a ritual, which may be simple or complex, and is often religious in nature. Sometimes, a weapon can be charged by leaving it lying in running water, or exposed to bright sunlight or to the light of the full moon. If the weapon contains a crystal, it's the crystal that gets charged.

* After use, the weapon needs to be ritually cleansed. This may be a simple act such as rinsing in running water, or it may need a prayer, or a complex ritual at the temple. The cleansing and the recharging are often done in the same ritual.

FICTIONAL COMPLICATIONS

* To be interesting, the weapon needs to have at least one weakness which causes difficulties for its user.

* After being ritually charged, the weapon works only for a specific period – perhaps for seven hours, or until the next new moon. After that period has passed, it may become inaccurate or less powerful, or stop working altogether.

* The weapon may only work in the hands of certain people: initiates of the order, male virgins, or post-menopausal crones. This can create interesting situations; for example, if it works only in the hands of a male virgin, the enemy may send a seductress.

* The weapon depends on the user's attitudes and beliefs. What if the weapon works only for a user whose religious faith is unshaken? What if it only works for someone who is free from fear?

* In many magic traditions, the knowledge of names plays an important role. Perhaps the weapon works only if the user knows the target's true name.

* In some magic traditions, especially modern ones, visualisation is important. Perhaps the weapon works only if the user can visualise the target's face.

* The weapon may work only if the user is in a state of altered consciousness (i.e. in a trance); this can be tricky in a battle.

* Magic spells often take time. The user needs time to raise magical energy and to direct her will at the desired outcome. In an urgent fight situation, time may be short.

* Magic requires intense concentration. Perhaps this weapon needs several seconds of undistracted concentration before every shot.

* The weapon may work only in the presence of a certain element (earth, air, fire, water). For example, the user must stand near an open fire, or the target must be close to running water, otherwise it won't work.

HOW TO DEFEAT A MAGICIAN

Magic is mental work, and the magician's main weapon is his mind. If your PoV is a magician who fights with magic, he may struggle to concentrate while fighting. If your PoV fights against a magician, she needs to ruin his concentration by creating distractions: talking, setting the curtains on fire, attacking him so fast he does not have time to think.

The best time to defeat a powerful magician is immediately after he has worked magic. Magic is mentally exhausting. It leaves the magician weak, tired and vulnerable. In this situation, your heroine can defeat the evil sorcerer. The post-magic exhaustion can also create interesting plot situations if your magician hero has exhausted himself protecting others with his magic, and left himself open to attack.

MAGIC IN WARFARE

The magicians who work in the field of warfare are specialists. They are not the same magicians who brew love potions and vanquish warts.

There may be one single magician who acts as consultant to the commander-in-chief of the country's armed forces, or each legion may have its own magician. There may also be specialist magician units, as there are medical and engineering units. Normally, these magicians are involved in the battle preparations rather than in the actual fighting. However, units of magician-soldiers (trained in magic as well as in fighting) are plausible. These are likely to be either elite troops or auxiliaries.

In real societies where magic is practised, the magic plays an important role in the run-up to the battle. Magicians fulfil the roles of consultants, astrologers, prophets, psychologists and priests. They determine an auspicious date for the battle, assure the soldiers that fortune is on their side, bless the banners, call the favour of the gods on the weapons, lead prayers and read animal entrails for omens.

Magicians cannot bestow invincibility. However, they can create protective spells which deflect bullets, arrows and sword blows. These do not offer perfect protection and are no substitute for a Kevlar vest. They merely reduce the number and severity of hits, so the protected warrior still needs to carry a shield and duck fast. The protection ritual takes time and energy to carry out. Shielding every soldier in an army of ten thousand with a protective spell is impractical. Perhaps only elite troops or only the officers are granted the treatment. This can lead to resentment among the grunt soldiers and create interesting sub-plots. Protection spells take time; in a sudden ambush, the magician does not have time to create the protection for the soldier who had counted on it. They also wear off fast, which allows you to build tension if the battle lasts longer than the fighters expected, or if one fight follows another.

For tips on how to write battle scenes, see Chapter 23.

BLUNDERS TO AVOID

* Magical weapons which can do anything, anywhere, any time

* Magicians who can do anything, anywhere, any time

CHAPTER 11: UNARMED COMBAT (HAND-TO-HAND FIGHTING)

In this chapter, you'll learn just enough about hand-to-hand fighting to write a believable scene.

Readers like hand-to-hand fighting because they perceive it as 'fair'. It also lends itself to entertaining scenes without bloodshed, and has the potential for erotic tension (see Chapter 27).

In a fight situation, people use the kind of fighting they are used to. There are two types: 'grappling' and 'striking'.

GRAPPLING

Martial arts: judo, wrestling, aikido, jiu jitsu, sambo, lucha libre, glima

Suitable for: entertaining fight scenes

Aim in lethal fight: choke (cut off the air) or strangle (cut off the blood supply to the brain), both achieved through pressure on the neck (they can also be used to render an opponent unconscious)

Words to use: grapple, wrestle, grab, twist, pull, pin, bend, roll, throw, toss, squeeze, press, choke, strangle

Holding the opponent down to the floor is called a 'pin' (verb: 'to pin'). In martial arts contests and show fighting, the opponent is usually pinned face-up. In a real fight, he is pinned face-down, because in this position he's helpless. For plot purposes, perhaps your hero has grappled the bad guy and is pinning him face down to the ground – and then the bad guy's buddy sneaks up and attacks the hero from behind.

Watch in action:

57

http://www.youtube.com/watch?v=jyM54qttw1I&feature=fvst

STRIKING

Martial arts: boxing, kick-boxing, karate, muay thai, capoeira, taekwondo

Suitable for: entertaining or gritty fight scenes

Aim in lethal fight: blow to head

Words to use: strike, hit, box, kick, punch, chop, slap, kick, slam, chop, hammer, pound

Watch in action:

http://www.youtube.com/watch?v=8l2nxe_Z4_g

MIXING MARTIAL ARTS

Some martial arts (e.g. krav maga) combine grappling and striking techniques. A skilled martial artist is probably an expert in either striking or grappling, but also has basic skills in the other.

If your hero or heroine has a background in martial arts, their fight skills are more plausible. Although you can mix martial arts in your scene, it's easier to write if you stick to just one group.

INVENTING A FANTASY MARTIAL ART

If your novel is set in a different society or world, you may want to invent a martial art.

Here are some pointers. The fictional martial art probably involves most (but not all) of these elements:

* Spiritual component. Almost every martial art has a strong spiritual (not necessarily religious) aspect. Connect it to the religious or philosophical traditions of your fantasy world.

* Non-violence. The aim is to avoid harming others. While capable of lethal violence, the proficient martial artist avoids using it. Of course, villainous characters may abuse their skill and enjoy the ability to inflict hurt.

* Mental focus. Body and mind are trained to work together. Concentration, focus and alertness are emphasised. Training may include mental exercises and, at advanced level, changing levels of consciousness.

* Small rituals. For example, bowing to the teacher before and after every lesson, bowing to the opponent before and after every fight. Each ritual has a reason.

* Strict hierarchy. The ranking is based on skills and experience. Everyone respects and obeys those of senior rank.

* Code of honour. The martial art defines and dictates honourable behaviour, both in practice and in real fighting, and sometimes in other aspects of life.

* Rules. Students are required to memorise and recite a set of rules and to abide by them at all times. These rules include the martial art's code of honour.

* Restricted admission. Only certain groups are allowed to learn and practice the martial art. For example, only females or only males, only members of a certain caste, ethnicity, nationality or tribe. Teaching outsiders may carry a penalty.

* Specialist technique. The focus is either on either grappling or striking moves. Within that movement group, the martial art is renowned for characteristic movements: high kicks or low kicks, angular or circular movements, direct or subtle strikes.

* Weapons. Training at advanced level includes mastery of weapons. The focus is on one specific weapon, which may be a simple object (staff), a traditional weapon (dagger, sword) or a weird weapon that's useless in ordinary people's hands but deadly if wielded by a trained practitioner. The martial artist considers this weapon an extension of his body, not an object to be used.

* Training from childhood. Practitioners may start learning as soon as they can walk, and the training continues for the whole lifetime.

* Practice. Everyone practices frequently, perhaps as a regular routine, e.g. every morning before breakfast.

* Body conditioning: A particular set of exercises serves to toughen certain body parts, for example striking a piece of wood wrapped with coarse rope, or thrusting fingers into a pile of small pebbles.

* Discipline. Students and practitioners are subjected to strict discipline, which may involve humiliation and penalties. They also practice a high degree of self-discipline.

* Drills. Certain movement sequences – based on actual fight situations – are practised over and over, by students on their own and by the whole class. Each movement sequence has a name; these may be colourful and reflect your fantasy world, e.g. 'The Eight-Legged Tiger' or 'Eagle Swooping From Mountain Top'.

* Exams. Students must prove themselves before passing to the next level. The exam includes theory (reciting rules), drills (assessed for technical correctness) and a series of fights against peers. For the fighting test, winning may be required, or it may be enough if the student stands up again for the next fight.

* Visual display of rank. Depending on seniority and skill level, practitioners may wear different coloured clothes, badges or belts.

* Special garments. Clothes of specific colours and cuts are worn for training and tournaments.

* Membership clues. Practitioners recognise other practitioners by certain words, gestures, garments or accessories. These may be known to the public, or secret.

* Tradition. The old ways are honoured and change is discouraged. Students may be required to memorise the history of the martial art. The founders may be worshipped. Tradition is taken so seriously that breaking from tradition causes strong inner and outer conflicts.

* Superiority. Many practitioners consider their martial art to be more honourable or more effective than other martial arts.

WHO WINS?

Three factors decide the outcome of an unarmed fight: Skill – Size – Ruthlessness.

The trained skilled fighter defeats the unskilled fighter. If both have the same level of skills, the bigger person wins. The more ruthless fighter also has an advantage.

Of these three, skill is the most important. A highly skilled fighter can overcome a much bigger, ruthless opponent. A petite girl can defeat a huge man if she has years of aikido training and he has none.

To make the outcome of the fight plausible, ensure that the winner has martial arts training.

More about this in Chapter 13.

BLUNDERS TO AVOID

* Professional assassins/bad guys/thugs who have little or no fight skills

* Protagonists who miraculously use fight skills they haven't previously acquired

CHAPTER 12: SELF-DEFENCE

Readers love self-defence scenes, especially if it's a woman defending herself against a man. You may want to insert a self-defence scene – or even a single self-defence paragraph – in your novel. Perhaps the heroine puts up a spirited fight before the kidnappers overpower her, or she wards off a lecher's forceful advances. In romance novels, the heroine may even fight off the hero – of course only at the beginning of the novel, before they've become allies. Near the end of the book, she's more likely to fight at the hero's side against the forces of evil.

When attacked, most victims go into a 'freeze' (See Chapter 14). To give your scene realism, you may like to include a freeze moment.

For many victims, the first reaction is either to search for reasons or to blame themselves: 'Why is this happening?' 'Why me?' 'It's my fault, because...', 'I should never have...' 'If only I hadn't...' and so on. By including such a thought, you can reflect reality. But don't allow your heroine to dwell on it, because this would make her appear a wimpy wuss in the readers' eyes. Maybe one single sentence serves the purpose. Instead, let her rapidly assess the situation.

ASSESSING THE DANGER

* How acute is the danger? (If the attacker pressing a gun to her temple, the danger is more acute than if he merely holds her in a bear grip. The less acute the danger, the more choices she has).

* What is at stake? (If material goods are at stake, for example, the attacker wants her wallet, she may decide to hand it over instead of risk her life fighting. But if he's an assassin hired to execute her, she must fight for her life.)

* Is this an opportunistic or a targeted attack? If the attacker is an opportunist who randomly picked a lone woman, any kind of resistance may be enough. Once he realises she's not the easy victim he thought, he'll leave off. But if he wants to kill her specifically, and has waited for this moment when he can get her – for example, a grieving father who has sworn vengeance on the doctor who failed to save his son – it won't be easy to drive him away.

* What are the chances of help arriving in time? If the attack happens near a busy thoroughfare, screaming for help may bring hordes of helpers eager to protect a woman. In this case, her best strategy may be to scream and to gain time until help arrives. But if it occurs in an isolated spot where nobody will hear her, where nobody may even find her corpse for months, she is on her own and must fight.

* How experienced is the attacker? If he is a first-timer trying it out, he may be insecure and slow to react. Then best strategy is to take control of the situation, to act rather than react. But if he's a routine serial killer or a professional assassin, she can't afford to make a mistake or she's dead. If she's a streetwise girl or a cop, she can read clues in his body language, in the way he holds the knife, in the sound of his voice, but the average attack victim may not be able to judge this well.

Don't spend many words on the assessment – two sentences may be enough – because the reader wants to move on to the Action.

SKILLED SELF-DEFENCE

If your heroine is trained in self-defence or martial arts, she has a whole range of techniques at her disposal. Half a year of martial arts training can be sufficient for a spirited defence.

She may knock the guy down. This is surprisingly easy to do for a skilled fighter, especially if the opponent is tall and thin. Suddenly finding himself on the floor, he'll spend several moments wondering what he's gotten himself into, and further moments scrambling to his feet. By this time, she has already escaped.

Here are some clips showing simulated attacks and how your heroine might respond:

http://www.youtube.com/watch?v=DGW7eVzulg0 (the attacker pushes the woman against the wall and chokes her from the front)

http://www.youtube.com/watch?v=QO2FEdtRi44&feature=related (a similar situation, with a different way out)

http://www.youtube.com/watch?v=WzkhvydILYY&feature=related (the attacker pushes her against a car and chokes her from behind)

http://www.youtube.com/watch?v=eM6Bpz6-dio (the attacker threatens the victim with a handgun)

http://www.youtube.com/watch?v=yH-vgvUEFbI (self-defence against a knife to the throat)

However, to pull these self-defence manoeuvres off, your heroine needs to know them, and she needs to have practised them many times – and not every woman is a martial artist or drilled in self-defence.

UNSKILLED SELF-DEFENCE

Your heroine can apply only the skills she possesses. A novice can't disable a thug with a roundhouse kick, and a Victorian damsel won't fell her attacker with an uppercut.

Fear may lend strength, but it doesn't grant implausible skills.

Here's the solution: the heroine performs a self-defence move which doesn't require prior training. Although it won't defeat the villain, it will buy her precious seconds during which she can escape from his clutches.

If you need ideas for a simple but effective and plausible self-defence tactic, perhaps one of these suggestions will suit your story:

1. She uses her feet. Attackers expect their victims to defend themselves with their hands, so they hold the victim in a way which prevents her from moving her arms. However, your heroine is clever: she stomps her heel down on his foot, preferably on the instep. This works especially well if she's wearing high heels. The pain makes him relax his grip, though only for a moment, so she may follow this with #2. The drawback is that she needs to hit his foot without first looking down.

2. She kicks him in the leg. This makes him stagger and loosen his grip for a moment. Depending on how he holds her, she can kick forwards, backwards or sideways. She can kick his shin, his calf, his knee, his thigh, or his crotch, as long as she kicks hard.

Her kick has more power if she first bends her leg and pulls her knee towards her torso and kicks from this position. (In martial arts lingo: 'she chambers her leg'). This allows her to kick stronger and higher, but it needs to be done quickly.

3. If she's shorter than her attacker, she sags against him as if in defeat, then suddenly straightens, ramming her head under his chin. This hurts her head, but it hurts his jaw a lot more. As he loosens his grip in pain and surprise, she breaks free.

4. If she has a hand free, she spreads the first and middle fingers and stabs them into his eyes. This blinds him temporarily, giving her time to escape. It doesn't work if he wears glasses.

The violence of this method makes it unsuitable for gentle forms of fiction, and the heroine should use it only against a bad guy, not against an honourable enemy or innocent prison guard.

5. She can go for his balls. Every woman knows that a man's privates are vulnerable, and if she can punch or squeeze him there (or, if his clothes are loose enough, grab, pull and twist), he'll probably be out of action long enough for her to make her escape.

However, men are aware of their vulnerability. Only a very stupid attacker would allow a female victim to grab his bits. Besides, this method is so over-used in fiction that it has become a predictable cliché. You could make it less predictable and more plausible by letting the heroine use her elbow or her knee.

6. She can use a skill from a different context, for example, from her hobby or her job, and adapt it as a self-defence manoeuvre. If her hobby is yoga, she can use her flexibility to slip out of her attacker's grasp. If she's a ballet dancer, she can fell him with a fouette. In real life, these would probably not work - but they feel realistic, because the heroine's special skill has been established.

7. She can grab something to use as a weapon. Perhaps there's a broomstick leaning against the wall, or she's holding a heavy shopping bag which she can swing and slam into the guy.

She can also use a tool of her trade as a weapon: the archaeologist may do something nifty with a trowel, the hair stylist with the curling iron, the gardener with the spade.

For more ideas on improvised weapons and how to use them, see Chapter 9.

KEEP IT SHORT

Since the aim of self-defence is to escape the danger, rather than to defeat an opponent, self-defence scenes tend to be very short. Often, they are just a paragraph within a larger scene.

BLUNDERS TO AVOID

* Heroines without previous training miraculously dispatching bad guys

* Bad guys who stand still so the heroine can hit their nuts

CHAPTER 13: STRENGTH, SKILL AND STRATEGY

Success in a fight depends on three factors: Strength - Strategy - SkillTo win a fight, your protagonist needs at least one of them. Otherwise, a good outcome is implausible.

STRENGTH

If two untrained fighters are matched in unarmed combat, the bigger, stronger one always wins.

Some people - especially men - are naturally strong. Strength increases with training (e.g. lifting weights, working out at the gym, a job involving physical labour). Sheer body mass also helps, especially in grappling-type fights (an obese woman can overpower a spindly man).

A fighter who has little muscle power (e.g. a dainty female) can sometimes use her other physical advantages (flexibility, agility). People with big muscles often lack flexibility. If your heroine has great flexibility thanks to daily stretches and yoga, she can use this in a wrestling match against an inflexible muscle-bound opponent.

In a dangerous situation, the body releases adrenalin into the bloodstream which gives extra strength. Your heroine may be able to accomplish feats of strength she couldn't do before - but don't overdo this: miracles are rare.

Strength is more important in unarmed combat than in armed fights. Some weapons need little strength (handguns), others need a lot (two-handed cleaving swords).

STRATEGY

Readers enjoy it when the protagonist outwits the opponent by cunning, resourcefulness and clever planning.

However, in a dangerous situation, fear paralyses the thinking, and during the fight, the brain is too busy to think anything.

To make the clever strategy plausible, your protagonist must plan it before the fight starts. If possible, it should be something he has done before, perhaps in a different context. For example, he may adapt something he's done during martial arts sparring, or learnt at cop school, or even part of a gymnastics routine or acrobatic act. The best strategy combines ingenuity with experience. As long as the strategy includes something the protagonist has done before, the scene is plausible.

SKILL

Readers like it when the protagonist wins with skills over brawn.

Skill comes from training and experience. People don't suddenly develop the ability to knock out an enemy. To make your fight scene plausible, make sure your fighters are trained. If possible, include martial arts or weapons training in their backstory. If your heroine has practised judo from the age of six, or if your hero learnt swordcraft as a young page in a nobleman's service, the reader will believe the fighting skills.

Establish this skill before it's needed in the fight scene. Weave a brief glimpse of those skills into another scene. Perhaps your heroine is practising karate katas in front of the mirror, or arranging her shooting trophies on the shelf, or giggling with her girlfriends over the women's self-defence workshop they've taken.

The bad guys can fight, too! The evil overlord is skilled with his weapon, and the henchmen in his employ are probably experienced assassins. The corrupt cops, dungeon guards, enemy warriors and ruthless thugs all know how to fight.

HOW MUCH TRAINING?

After half a year of martial arts training, two sessions per week, your heroine is able to defend herself against an unarmed untrained attacker.

Any martial art will do - aikido, judo, karate, wrestling, krav maga etc - as long as she has practised diligently. Tai chi is less suitable; although it's a martial art, most classes focus more on energy flow and balance than fighting. You may want to choose a martial art of which you have some experience, even if yours is at basic level. Self-defence classes can be perfect for fictional heroines, because they teach highly effective tricks in a short time.

However, if the bad guys are skilled fighters (many real-life bad guys are), half a year at martial arts school won't take your heroine far. If the plot requires that she defeats a fighting-skilled opponent, I recommend giving her a lot more training. Perhaps she has studied her martial art since childhood, practises it with enthusiasm, and participates in competitions. Then almost anything is plausible.

The training does not necessarily have to be advanced. The fighter who knows only five basic moves but has practised them to perfection will perform better than the person who knows five hundred but hasn't practised them properly.

Weapons need experience, too. The more experience the fighter has, the more believable is his victory. It's implausible that someone picks up a gun or a sword for the first time and successfully kills an enemy. He needs to have practised with the weapon - the more, the better.

WHERE DOES THE EXPERIENCE COME FROM?

The training can be formal (police academy, martial arts dojo) or informal (children's play-fighting, street brawls). Either way, it has to be believable. Is it plausible that this particular person learnt this particular kind of fighting in this particular way?

In a contemporary novel, it's easy to come up with some kind of training in your protagonist's backstory.

In a historical novel, this can be trickier. Certain weapons were the prerogative of certain classes, and people from different classes could neither afford those weapons nor access the training. In many periods and societies, women didn't fight at all, so you need to think creatively to find a way to give your heroine weapons or martial arts training. For more about female fighters in historical periods, see Chapter 15.

MUSCLE MEMORY

Fight skills work best if the protagonist has practised the same moves over and over. A good self-defence workshop makes the student drill each move dozens of times. In martial arts, students repeat the same movements thousands of times, until they can do them without thinking. When a fight situation occurs, the martial artist automatically applies the appropriate move.

The training doesn't have to be recent. In an emergency, the brain and the muscles remember what they practised years ago. For example: An old lady gets attacked by a thug in the park. Without thinking, she tosses him over her shoulder with a judo throw. She hasn't practised that move - or any judo - for sixty years. But her brain remembers the judo training from her teens, and automatically applies it.

BLUNDERS TO AVOID

* Implausible fight skills... as if the situation instantly granted the Regency damsel a black belt in karate

* Everyone has a black belt... as if those accessories were sold in bulk at a discount store

CHAPTER 14: PSYCHOLOGICAL BARRIERS

People who need to fight often aren't prepared to fight. When faced with a threat, a person without fight experience may simply freeze, unable to move.

RELUCTANCE TO FIGHT

Many humans, especially women, have a natural aversion to violence. They don't want to hurt another person. They are unable to use violence, even if that other person is about to hurt them.

For example: a woman gets attacked by a rapist. She has one hand free and knows she can stop him by stabbing her fingers into his eyes - but she can't bring herself to do it. Not wanting to inflict injury, she hesitates... and then it's too late.

Or she hits immediately, but only at half-strength, and then she waits to check what effect the hit had. Her experienced opponent, on the other hand, hits immediately at full strength.

MARTIAL ARTS VS STREET FIGHTING

Martial artists, even if they are used to sparring, have won trophies, have earned belts and excel in competitions, sometimes fail in real fights. When suddenly confronted with violence, they need to make a mental and emotional shift from the civilised, respectful, rule-abiding atmosphere of the ring, to the brutal, ruthless reality of the street. They can't adapt quickly enough.

Once the psychological barrier is broken (i.e. the protagonist has been in a real fight), she can adapt quickly in future fights.

In an 'entertaining' fight scene, these considerations don't matter. But in 'gritty' fight scenes, they matter a lot. If in doubt, give your protagonist actual fight experience in addition to skills.

THE FREEZE

When confronted with sudden danger, most people's instinctive response is to stop moving and stay absolutely still.

This is actually a useful survival instinct stemming from pre-history. When faced with sudden danger, the human has three choices: fight, flight, or freeze. In pre-history, freezing was often the wisest choice, because a large predator animal loses interest in prey which doesn't move. An unarmed man can't defeat a sabre-toothed tiger, nor can he outrun it, but he can pretend to be dead so the tiger leaves him alone.

In a danger situation, the choice between fight, flight and freeze has to be made instantly. Under pressure, humans often make an unfortunate choice. Since most would not have the courage to stand still when the sabre-toothed tiger comes, nature has wired freezing as the default option into the human brain.

When faced with a menacing threat, the human often gets locked into a freeze and can't run, move or shout even if he wanted to.

This mental state is often pleasant: instead of panic, the person experiences comfortable, fuzzy warmth, and may even feel like he is floating. There may be a roaring in his ears, but otherwise, sounds are faint. Everything seems to happen in slow motion, with no urgency to act. The thinking is highly illogical, but can feel crystal clear at the time.

Unfortunately, the freeze is not helpful when the attacker is a frenzied axe-wielding psychopath. Then fleeing or fighting would be better options. This means the fiction character has to break out of the instinctive freeze and start fighting.

Novices and seasoned veterans both can get the freeze, but the experienced fighter can usually snap out of it in a fraction of a second, while the novice may stay stuck in it until it is too late.

The freeze has no place in a purely entertaining fight scene. In a realistic or mixed scene, it can add realism, especially if the person is inexperienced in fighting. However, readers despise characters who stay in a freeze for a long time. If it's the heroine, hero or main villain, I recommend letting them snap out of the freeze fast.

If possible, write it avoiding the word 'freeze' because the phrase 'He/she froze' is a cliché (an overused phrase). Instead, describe what it feels like, for example:

She stared at the knife, transfixed by the diamond sparkles of sunlight on the blade. Then she snapped out of the spell and slammed his arm aside.

CHAPTER 15: FEMALE FIGHTERS

In this chapter, you'll learn how to create a spunky heroine who kicks male butt and is real. We'll look at reader expectations, and at the differences between male and female fight styles.

Bear in mind that not all women are the same. I'm discussing what is typical for women - your heroine or villainess may be different.

READER EXPECTIONS

Until a few decades ago, readers liked heroines who offered only passive resistance, who waited patiently until the male hero came to their rescue, and who watched from the sidelines as the hero fought against the villain.

Today's readers expect the heroine to get involved in the fighting. Moreover, they expect her to fight with courage and skill. If the hero rescues the heroine in one scene, then she'll rescue him right back in the next, and during the Climax, they fight side by side to defeat the minions of evil.

If there's fighting to be done, the heroine has to get involved. Watching from the sidelines, screaming or fainting are no longer options.

PHYSICAL DIFFERENCES

The average woman is shorter than the average man. This makes it more difficult to wield a long sword, or to slam something down on her opponent's head.

More importantly, the average woman has less muscle strength than the average man, which is a real disadvantage during unarmed fighting. The modern heroine can be quite strong, especially if she has built strength by working out in the gym, by lifting weights, by practising sports, or by working in a job which involves physical labour.

A woman who works out can plausibly be stronger than a male couch potato. However, if a woman and a man both exercise a lot, the man is much stronger.

To build muscles, the human body needs male hormones, and the female body has a limited amount of those, which limits the mass of muscle she can have. A well-trained female body has visible muscles on arms, shoulders, abdomen, legs etc. - but it doesn't have bulging muscle balloons. Those are a physical impossibility, unless she takes male hormone supplements (as female bodybuilders do).

If you're writing historical fiction, giving your heroine any kind of physical strength can be tricky. In periods when sport activities were considered harmful to female health, and when the ideal of female beauty was a frail weak body, women of the upper classes didn't have physical strength. You may want to mention that your heroine is an eager horsewoman or an accomplished dancer, because those were often the only socially accepted physical activities, and they could give her considerable fitness and strength.

On the other hand, a woman of the poorer classes could not afford keeping her body frail in fashionable idleness. The peasant, the housemaid, the washerwoman had to labour from dawn to dusk, often doing strenuous physical work. These women naturally developed muscles, and might plausibly be stronger than an idle gentleman.

Another disadvantage for the female fighter is that her bones are more fragile than a man's. This is especially important in striking-type martial arts such as boxing. A male fist smashing into a female face can cause serious devastation, whereas if a woman slugs a man's jaw, she may break her own fingers. An experienced female martial artist knows this, and will target the part of the man's body where the bones are thin (for example, his nose) or which are not protected by bones (his throat, abdomen, groin).

These physical disadvantages mean that the reader's sympathies lie with the female fighter. If your heroine fights a man, you don't need to work hard to make the reader root for her.

Do women have physical advantages over men? Yes, some, although those are minor.

The centre of gravity in a woman's body is lower than in a man's, which makes it harder to knock her off balance. Women's bodies also tend to be more flexible, a natural advantage which is increased by the type of exercise women do - stretching, yoga, gymnastics - and gives women an advantage in grappling fights because they can more easily slip out of holds.

A woman's small size can also work to her advantage if her opponent has only ever trained with male opponents. His big hands may not get a proper grip on a woman's slender limbs.

PSYCHOLOGICAL DIFFERENCES

I'm talking about the differences between average women and average men. Not every point applies to every individual. You know your heroine; use what fits her personality.

Typically, women are less aggressive than men. This applies especially to the Suspense and Start sections. While many men are roused to fight at the slightest provocation, women are not so easily provoked. Indeed, women usually try other options first - such as pleading, negotiating, or developing a non-violent strategy.

You may like to show your heroine being more level-headed than her male companions. You can also create realism by letting your heroine talk before she fights, perhaps trying to dissuade her opponent from fighting. When negotiation fails, she can fight as ferociously as a man.

The non-aggressive stance may change instantly and drastically if a woman's children are in danger. In defence of their offspring, some mothers become tigresses.

In Chapter 14, we looked at psychological barriers. Women have a greater aversion to violence than men, and many (though not all) dislike inflicting hurt. You can use this concept in several ways: Your heroine's preferred fight style may be non-bloody, she may knock out her enemies rather than kill them, and she may take captives rather than commit slaughter. If she fights as part of a team, she may argue with her male comrades about how much violence to apply.

In a gritty fight scene, the fight-inexperienced heroine's qualms about violence may cost her precious moments.

Many men have qualms about hurting a woman, and may not apply full force against her. A woman can exploit this reluctance.

When a woman feels threatened, she'll instinctively grab something to use as a weapon: a crystal vase, a flower pot, a cooking spoon. This reflex is stronger in women than in men.

SOCIETY'S ATTITUDES

In most cultures, society emphasises and generalises gender differences. Your heroine may have encountered attitudes like these:

"Most women are weaker than most men, therefore all women are weak, and a woman who isn't weak is not a woman."

"Women don't like violence, therefore women cannot be warriors/soldiers/police officers/bodyguards."

"A woman who enjoys fighting is a sinner/a monster/a witch."

"Women's bones are fragile, therefore a woman must not engage in sports or martial arts."

"Men are stronger than women, which proves that God wants women to submit to men. Therefore, a woman who defends herself against male aggression is disobeying God."

Even in modern Western society, some people think it's bad for a woman's character if she can defend herself against a man.

Such attitudes are a huge obstacle to a woman's training and progress. She may have had to compromise. For example, the modern heroine may have yearned to study karate, but settled for judo because her strict macho father considered it more appropriate for a girl. Your Victorian heroine may have dreamed of target shooting with firearms, but settled for archery, because this was the only martial sport to which females were occasionally admitted.

SKILLS AND BACKSTORY

To compensate for disadvantages in height and muscle strength, your heroine needs skill and strategy.

In unarmed combat, it's perfectly plausible that a petite female wipes the floor with a brawny male if she has better fighting skills.

Remember to establish the kind and level of her skills before the fight, and make them plausible for the period and society she lives in. For a contemporary novel, it's easiest if you simply give her a martial art which she has practised from childhood. Alternatively, she could have learnt martial arts or weapons skills as part of her on-the-job training, for example, as a soldier or police officer.

Perhaps she learnt fighting in a previous job. For example, she may have worked as an erotic wrestler or catfighter to finance her college studies. More about this in Chapter 27.

Although she may no longer perform as a wrestler or catfighter, it's worth considering the moral issues involved, and measuring them against her values. She may have had not the slightest qualms about these performances, or she may have had qualms but considered fighting less immoral than stripping or prostitution. Or she may have done it for only a year, felt guilty about it, and tried to hide it from her current respectable employers and prudish fiancé.

If you're writing historical fiction set in a period when women didn't fight, it gets tricky. Your heroine couldn't have attended a martial arts dojo or a shooting range. Perhaps she grew up among boys, and did a lot of play-fighting with them until puberty. Or perhaps she was an only child, and her father treated her as a substitute son and gave her a boy's training.

INEXPERIENCED FEMALE FIGHTERS

A woman who is not trained in martial arts, and who has no fighting experience, instinctively does one of these:

1. Try to talk herself out of the situation (attempt to persuade her attacker to let her go)

2. Grab something to use as a weapon. See the section on 'Improvised Weapons' in Chapter 9.

3. Use her hands to try to break free.

4. Pull hair.

5. Scratch.

In a serious fight, hair pulling and scratching are mostly ineffective. The only advantage is that when police find her corpse, the hair on the carpet and the skin under her fingernails contain the attacker's DNA.

DIFFERENT FIGHTING STYLES

Female martial artists are often very technically precise fighters. Men can perform a sloppy manoeuvre and it will work because of their muscle power. Women need to get it absolutely right to make it work. Therefore, female martial artists learn the importance of technical precision early on, which stands them in good stead at advanced level.

Women observe their opponents more than men do. They assess the opponent's strengths, weaknesses, habits, and use them to their advantage. Females are often strategic fighters.

In a typical female/male fight, the man makes the first move, the woman the second. Men start punching/hitting/grabbing immediately. Women tend to wait for the man to make the first move, and then respond to it, often using his own momentum against him. However, this applies only to unarmed fighting. In a gunfight, she can't afford to let him have the first shot. It also doesn't apply if the woman is an assassin or crazed with vengeance.

FEMALE CURVES OF AROUSAL

In a fight situation, the brain releases a mix of chemicals - adrenaline, hormones, neurotransmitters and such - into the bloodstream. These give the fighter a boost of courage, strength, stamina and focus, but they reduce the ability to think rationally and to feel compassion, and when they wear off, they can leave the fighter wobbly, weepy and weak.

Women get almost the same chemical mix as men - but at a different time. For men, it often happens at the slightest trigger, a sharp spike of arousal which builds quickly but doesn't last long. For women, the arousal happens less often, builds far more slowly, and lasts longer. This is similar to the different curves of sexual arousal.

In practice, this means that a man may fight at the slightest provocation, quickly get intense, irrational and violent, and finish fighting as soon as he's won. A woman, on the other hand, may be slow to engage in fighting, her initial strikes may be cautious and reluctant, and at the beginning of the fight, she's still level-headed. As the fight goes on, she becomes more and more violent and loses all rational thought and compassion, and once she's in full flow, she may not stop even when her opponent begs for mercy.

You can use these different curves of arousal if a female and a male character are fighting side by side, for example if the heroine and the hero are on a date and get attacked by thugs.

While she still tries to avoid the problem or to talk the attackers out of their plan, the hero is already using his weapon or his fists. He has already landed several blows before she joins the fighting. By the time his adrenaline spike wears off and he loses his strength and accuracy, she's at her best and fights like a berserker. In the Aftermath, her chemicals will subside slowly, making her feel wobbly and weepy, while his have already subsided, and he is rational again.

If they're an established team - say, two police officers who have been partnered for years - they'll be aware of each other's different curves of arousal, and use them to advantage. For example, when a dangerous situation arises, she can count on him to respond quickly to the threat, while he can rely on her to keep her head and develop a strategy. When he feels his chemicals wearing off and he can no longer box with the same strength, he can rely on her to take over. After the fight, when her chemicals subside and she's shaking and has tears in her eyes, she can count on him to distract their colleagues so they won't see her cry.

If you have a female villain renowned for brutality, her violent streak will manifest more intensely as the fight goes on.

WOMEN AND WEAPONS

Weapons are equalisers. Physical strength, important in unarmed combat, matters less if the fighters are armed. A slender frail girl can pull a trigger as easily as a big brawny bloke. However, some weapons require height or strength. It would take an unusually brawny woman to wield a two-handed medieval greatsword.

When choosing a weapon for your historical heroine, choose something she may plausibly own, and for which a woman of that period can plausibly have training. For example, in the Victorian era, weapons-handling was generally considered inappropriate for a woman, but archery was borderline acceptable. This makes it more likely that your heroine is a skilled archer than a skilled rifle shooter.

Daggers, handguns, bows, slings and staffs can be good choices for fictional heroines.

FEMALE SOLDIERS

In most cultures, organised warfare is a man's job.

Scholars have come up with interesting hypotheses about the reasons, mostly variations of 'men are expendable, women are precious'. The men are soldiers; the women either stay at home or they serve in non-combatant roles (cooks, instructors, administrators, nurses).

However, there have been instances of female warriors throughout history. Usually, women and men fight in segregated units. The female units often have a special function (e.g. to protect the royal family, to defend the temple), and they may be specialists in a certain kind of fighting or with certain weapons (e.g. light skirmishers, mounted archers).

Mixed gender armies are rare, although there are a few reports from early historical times (i.e. Celts fighting against Romans). Mixed gender armies are most likely during desperate defence situations, when there aren't enough men.

When creating a mixed-gender or all-female army, consider these questions: are the women amateurs or professionals? Are they deployed for special missions? Are they specialists in a particular kind of fighting? What are the consequences of pregnancy and motherhood? (Maybe pregnant soldiers are assigned to non-combat tasks? Maybe warriors swear an oath of celibacy on joining, and mothers get expelled from the legion?)

CLOTHING AND ARMOUR

Female fighters on book covers, in comic books and in the movies often look like models for erotic fetish wear, clad in high boots and chainmail bras, with bare bellies and long flowing hair. This is highly implausible, so don't dress your heroine in these costumes.

Thigh-high boots restrict the leg movement. Bare thighs would be stupid, because so much blood pumps through the thigh that a single slash can make a person bleed to death. Your female warrior will keep her thighs covered, preferably with something sturdy such as leather, but at the very least with fabric. The same applies to the belly. Throughout most of history, an abdominal wound meant certain death, so no warrior would leave her belly exposed.

A chainmail bra is heavy, pulls the breasts downwards, adds little protection, and can get in the way of her own weaponry. It serves no conceivable purpose (except maybe to distract an opponent who happens to be a chainmail fetishist). Your heroine will support her breasts to avoid painful bouncing. In the modern era, she'll use a strong sports bra. In a historical period, she'll either tie her breasts tight with a fabric bandage (tighter than she wears for everyday life) or support them with some kind of leather corselet. Large breasts may get into the way of the sword arm, so she may tie one breast so tightly that it's almost flat (which can lead to rumours that female warriors amputate their breasts).

Long flowing hair is also impractical, since it falls into the face and restricts the vision. She's more likely to tie it into a ponytail, to plait it or to pin it under a helmet.

If she's a professional warrior or a frequent fighter, she owns a set of clothes designed for fighting. These give freedom of movement and probably also protection from weapons. For a professional warrior, check out the costume of male fighters of your chosen period, and invent a female variation. For information about armour, see Chapter 20. If her fighting is secret (for example, because she's an assassin, or because she leads a double life), she'll design a costume which looks like ordinary women's dress but can adapt in an instant to a fighting outfit.

You can also create interesting situations when your heroine has to fight unprepared, in unsuitable clothes. Perhaps she gets attacked outside the nightclub, and is wearing high heels and pencil skirt, which makes karate kicks difficult.

Here's an example of a beautiful picture of a beautiful warrior maiden whose costume is as impractical as it gets:

http://Calandrastudio.com/Calandra_Studio.html (the main picture in the middle of the top row - the blonde in the chainmail bikini)

And for a bit of fun, a tongue-in-cheek video about female fantasy armour:

http://www.collegehumor.com/video/6550847/female-armor-sucks

BLUNDERS TO AVOID

* The heroine performs feats for which she does not have plausible strength (e.g. a dainty girl swinging a greatsword)

* The heroine displays skills which a woman of her period and station could not have acquired

* Female warriors dressing for battle in chainmail bras, breechcloths and little else... as if they couldn't wait to be gutted by enemy swords

CHAPTER 16: MALE FIGHTERS

This chapter aims to help female writers write about male fighters. For a woman who has had a feminine upbringing, it can be difficult to put herself into the shoes of a male character whose instincts differ from hers, and for whom fighting was a normal part of growing up.

Of course, the suggestions in this chapter are generalisations, applying to most but not all men. Your hero or your villain may be different.

The biggest difference happens during the build-up to the fight - which probably covers the Suspense section of your scene. When gearing up for a fight, men use more posturing and fewer words than women.

DIALOGUE

While women use a lot of verbal arguing (arguing, explaining, accusing, allocating blame and hurling hysterical insults) before they use physical violence, men exchange just a few lines of terse dialogue, and then the fists talk.

Men's dialogue lines are short, laconic, and terse. Taunts are often phrased as questions and may include references to reproductive body parts. The whole pre-fight dialogue may consist of both men hurling taunting questions at each other.

Here are typical female and male dialogue lines for the build-up to a brawl.

Female examples

"It's your fault, because if you hadn't first done this-and-that, I wouldn't have had to resort to so-and-so, and then the bad thing wouldn't have happened."

"But at the meeting last week, you said you would do such-and-such. You can't just turn around and do so-and-so now."

"That's unfair to everyone, and I couldnt possibly let you get away with it."

"Unless you promise never to do that again, I have no choice but to use force."

"I'm giving you once last chance to apologise. Don't say I haven't warned you."

Male examples

"Are you calling me a liar?"

"Where's your courage now?"

"Prove it."

"Take it back."

"Bastard."

BODY LANGUAGE

Before men start fighting, they communicate a lot through body language, especially posture. Some of this is conscious, some is subconscious. The male PoV character consciously makes some postural gestures, and he observes the other man's posture shifts as well.

Each man tries to impress and intimidate his rival, giving him a chance to back out without fighting.

Here are some typical male body language cues shortly before fists fly:

* Standing with legs apart, elbows out to the side, shoulders squared, chin thrust forward and up, chest inflated and turned full front to his opponent, piercing stare. These cues are intended to make him look bigger and badder, and to claim larger space. He may also hook his hands into his belt, framing his genitals (sending the signal 'my macho is bigger than your macho').

* There may be signs that a man is readying his body for a fight, for example by subtly stretching his neck or spine.

* Often, one of the men steps close up to the other, invading the other man's space. If that guy steps back, he's the loser, and the fight won't happen. If the guy doesn't step back, the first man invades his space with touch, for example, shoving his shoulder. If that's tolerated, the one who has touched has won. More often, the other guy responds to the shoulder-shove with a punch, and the fight is on.

You can combine body language clues with dialogue in the Suspense section. Here are some examples:

Jim squared his shoulders. "Are you calling me a liar?"

Bob braced his legs. "Where is your courage now?"

"You'll regret this." Olaf balled his fists.

SKILLS

Practically all men possess fighting skills, whether they have had formal training or not. While little girls are forbidden to fight and get punished for transgressions, boys are usually encouraged. Thus, males learn the basics of fighting quickly, and most men know how to apply a wrestling hold or throw a punch.

When writing a scene from a male point of view, keep in mind that basic fighting techniques are routine for him, and he doesn't need to think about them. Female writers often get this wrong. After researching basic technique, they explain it step by step. *(Rotating the hand from the wrist until it was in a horizontal position with the back of the hand in a straight line with the arm, and curling his fingers around his thumb to avoid fracturing that digit, Jim moved his fist forward at high speed. The fist connected with the man's jaw. Jim withdrew the fist immediately, holding it before his face to protect himself against the inevitable counter attack.)* For a man - who probably learnt to box in his playground days - it would be better to write simply *He punched the guy's jaw* or *He slammed his fist into the guy's jaw.*

Many men also have formal training in fighting skills. In many cultures, serious weapons training is part of every boy's education, at least among the upper classes. Fighting with or without weapons is considered a suitable male sport. Fathers and uncles enjoy passing their fight skills to the boys of their families. In addition, many men spend some time serving in their countries' armed forces.

You don't need much imagination to explain why your hero is a skilled fighter, or to spend many words on back-story to make it plausible. All you need to give the reader is a brief glimpse of a photo of him in infantry uniform or of the hunting trophies displayed on his study wall. You could also show him cleaning his revolver or polishing his sword during a dialogue scene.

MEN AND THEIR WEAPONS

Men, especially macho types, often have a special relationship with their weapon: very personal, almost intimate. The weapon reflects the man's self-image and symbolises his masculinity - especially if it's remotely phallic-shaped, like a gun, a dagger, a sword or a mace.

The hero may spend his leisure hours lovingly repairing, oiling, polishing his weapon. When several men get together, they often compare their weapons (with the conversation centred around 'mine is bigger/longer/thicker/harder/better than yours'), and they brag about their weapon handling skill (how often they've scored).

If the heroine admires the hero's weapon, he'll be delighted to display it to her in its full glory. However, she had better not grab it uninvited.

MALE CURVES OF AROUSAL

In men, fighting instincts are aroused more often and faster than in women. The release of the chemical mix (adrenaline, neurotransmitters and hormones) into the bloodstream happens at the slightest provocation. This is why men - especially young men who have not yet learnt to control their urges - fight more frequently than women, and why male fists fly when females are still negotiating.

A man's fighting arousal ends faster than a woman's. Typically, all it takes is for the other man to surrender, and he'll stop. While she is still battering her helpless enemy with ever-increasing fury, he has already slapped his opponent on the back and bought him a drink at the bar.

MEN AGAINST WOMEN

Most men are reluctant to hurt a woman. This instinct is hard-wired into men, and even the villain will hesitate before striking the heroine. When men fight against women, they hit less hard than they would hit a man.

Even martial arts schools which pride themselves on gender equality have unwritten rules for protecting women. For example, some karate schools consider it dishonourable to do thigh kicks on a female. Thigh kicks are extremely painful, and they hurt men just the same as they hurt women. However, women are allowed to thigh-kick men, but not the other way round. There is no biological reason for sparing women - only the sense of chivalry hard-wired into those guys.

Of course, a ruthless woman can take advantage of the man's chivalry. While he's still hesitating, she knocks him down.

BLUNDERS TO AVOID

* Men talking like women in the build-up to a brawl

* Over-explaining basic fight moves

CHAPTER 17: ANIMALS AND WERES

HOW ANIMALS FIGHT

Although claws and teeth have weapon-like effects, you may find it easier to think of the animal fight as hand-to-hand combat. The style of most mammals resembles the grappling-type fighting; bird fights can be similar to the striking kind.

To make animal fight scenes realistic, watch wildlife documentaries, especially the sections which feature animals hunting, attacking, defending their young, disputing territory, or fighting over mates.

Watch animals in action

Here are some YouTube clips which may serve as inspiration:

http://www.youtube.com/watch?v=pb6Rke7jiTc&playnext=1&list=PL4FE9EE6C8DA6BA97 (musk ox vs wolves)

http://www.youtube.com/watch?v=ak2SQiRiA6g&feature=related (lion vs bull)

http://www.youtube.com/watch?v=XV7FLh7Bh-0 (snake vs snake)

http://www.youtube.com/watch?v=Rt94whY-X94 (hyena clan fight)

http://www.youtube.com/watch?v=NvoyMq84GO0 (lion vs lion)

http://www.youtube.com/watch?v=tufnqWNP9AA&feature=related (eagle vs eagle)

http://www.youtube.com/watch?v=1q9vx-CBueU (wolf vs wolf)

http://www.youtube.com/watch?v=RzfYsIC8ufs&playnext=1&list=PL4FE9EE6C8DA6BA97 (bear vs wolves)

http://www.youtube.com/watch?v=D_PHs-kbypo (tiger vs lion)

http://www.youtube.com/watch?v=-o7nLZWyinI&feature=relmfu (crocodile vs shark)

Pay special attention to the 'body language' and movements preceding the fight, when they strike poses to intimidate a rival, argue over the carcass of a kill, lie in ambush, stalk their prey, or get ready to defend their cubs. A couple of sentences showing the postures and movements preceding the fight add authenticity.

ANIMAL POV

If you're writing from the animal's point of view, use animal senses. In many animals, the sense of smell is far more developed than in humans. They can locate potential prey and note potential threats by scent, often from a considerable distance.

Predator animals react strongly to the scent of blood. Once an opponent is injured, the PoV may experience overwhelming reactions.

WERES

When a human turns into an animal, he acquires that animal's instincts. Is that animal mostly 'prey' or is it mostly 'predator'? This determines the fighting style.

Sensory perceptions also change. Once a human changes into an animal, he may get a sharper sense of hearing and a much keener sense of smell. This affects how he notes threats and how he reacts to them, how he responds to the sight and smell of blood, and how he fights.

In legend and in paranormal fiction, it usually takes a silver bullet to kill a were. It's possible to cast silver bullets, and to shoot them from a normal gun, as long as the size and shape of the bullets fits the gun. However, silver bullets are less accurate than normal ones. This can cause interesting challenges for the shooter who may need to get closer to the target than usual, or to fire several shots.

For originality, consider using something other than silver bullets. If the slaying of a were requires silver in its flesh, how about a silver arrowhead? Maybe a silvered spear-tip or a silvered dagger-point?

ANIMALS AS WEAPONS

Dogs

Dogs have strong fighting instincts and can be trained easily. This makes them potential weapons for humans. Hunting dogs, guard dogs and attack dogs are all trained to fight, and some historical armies had dog units. An individual human may have a ferocious dog fighting at his side, or a handler may command half a dozen dogs at once.

Choose one of the breeds used as police dogs or guard dogs: Giant Schnauzer, German Shepherd, Doberman Pinscher, Belgian Malinois, Airedale, Belgian Tervuren, Belgian Shepherd, Rottweiler.

Alternatively, hunting dogs could also be trained to fight.

Horses

Horses are not natural fighters, because their instincts drive them to flee rather than to attack.

Even most warhorses don't fight. They have been trained to stay calm in battle (the noises and smells would drive ordinary horses to panic), but not to fight.

A horse can be trained to fight - it may pivot on its hind legs so the front hooves become deadly weapons - but this requires a horse of exceptional intelligence, exceptional temperament, and exceptional courage. Such a horse may be precious, and most likely be owned by a rich knight or a royal war leader.

Units of fighters on horseback are called 'cavalry'. They are often skirmishers or archers. A massed cavalry charge against foot soldiers can be devastating.

When faced with a cavalry attack, ranged weapons work best - guns, stone slings, throwing spears, bows and arrows, to prevent them from getting close.

Horses are vulnerable, especially their legs. Armies expecting a cavalry charge may use traps, trip wires, and half-buried spikes to injure the approaching animals. Caltrops are balls with metal spikes, laid out on the ground so the horses will step on them and get injured. A simpler version consists of balls of thorny twigs. Another method is to set a row of spears diagonally into the ground, tip pointing forward. Most horses simply won't charge a mass of pointy sticks. However, all these defences work only if the fighters have time to prepare them.

In close-up fighting, the soldier on foot has almost no chance against the mounted fighter. The rider has the advantage of height and can slam his mace or sword down on the standing fighter, while the foot soldier can't even reach the rider's body.

If the plot requires that a single fighter on foot wins in close combat against a mounted warrior, give him a long lance. This allows him to attack the horse while staying out of the rider's immediate reach, or to thrust it upwards into the rider's body.

If the fighter on foot is armed with a dagger or sword, his best strategy is to injure one of the horse's legs severely, so the horse collapses and the rider loses his advantage. However, he needs to be quick, because the rider isn't going to sit still and watch while the man below him attacks the horse.

If the horseman's weapon is the sword, then the foot fighter will try to get on the shield side of the horse, away from the sword's reach.

The cost of buying and maintaining a horse makes it an expensive piece of 'equipment'. In many societies, the cavalry was made up of members of the wealthy upper classes.

Finding food and water for a horse - let alone for hundreds of horses - can be problematic and create interesting plot situations.

Elephants

Because of their size and strength, elephants have been used by historical armies as the ancient equivalent of tanks. They can trample enemies (although this is not in their nature; they need to be trained), and pull down walls and defences. The mere sight of elephants can create panic among the enemy army. From the back of elephants, archers can shoot arrows down at the enemy.

However, elephants need huge amounts of food and water, and supplying those may be difficult. Sometimes, elephants stampede through their own armies, causing terrible devastation. Shrill noises and the sight of fire can drive elephants into panic. Another problem is that elephants dislike the smell of other animals, and other animals dislike theirs, so the cavalry horses and the elephants need to be kept at a distance.

Other animals

In a fantasy world, it is plausible that humans use a variety of animals for fighting, especially animals which are natural predators and those which are easily trained. Even animals which cannot be trained may attack the enemy if they have been starved and tormented into aggression beforehand.

FIGHTING AGAINST AN ANIMAL

In a human versus animal fight, the animal - probably 'armed' with claws, beak or fangs - often has the advantage over the unarmed human.

Your character's best bet may be to avoid the fight by hiding or fleeing. Sometimes it helps to curl into a defensive ball and remain motionless. Running is also a good option, but most animals are faster. He can try to reach ground the animal can't reach, e.g. crawling into a narrow space where the big beast doesn't fit, or climbing up a tree if the animal can't climb.

If the plot requires that the human fights and wins, give him a weapon. Amazing feats have been achieved by humans fighting off lions, tigers, bears and other dangerous beasts with a knife. Those incidents are rare, but within the realms of the possible.

Make it plausible by researching where the animal's vulnerable spots are. Hunters are good people to ask about this.

If you can't obtain the right information, or if the animal is a fantasy creature, here are some pointers:

Large animals often have thick skulls which resist blows with rocks and sledgehammers, and blades can't penetrate. The chest is often covered by thick, sometimes scaled, armour-like skin deflecting stabs and cuts, and even if the blade penetrates the skin, it may not get beyond the bones.

A better option is to stab the animal in the side, if possible behind the front flank. If the blade is long enough, it can reach the heart and kill.

If the blade is short, even a series of stabs may not stop a big, enraged animal.

Most animals have vulnerable throats, where the human can stab or slash to kill. A stab in the eye is also effective, but it's not easy to hit this small moving target during a fight.

A human who has single-handedly fought and killed a dangerous beast may be celebrated by his people. He may be given a name reflecting this, such as Ben the Bearslayer, He-Who-Kills-Lions or Tara Dragondeath, and will probably wear something from the defeated animal as an accessory for the rest of his life, e.g. a cape trimmed with the wolf's pelt, a necklace of grizzly teeth or earrings made from shimmering dragon scales.

BLUNDERS TO AVOID

* The heroine's horse kicking to defend her against an attacker

* Animals fighting the way humans fight

* Predator animal PoV not responding to smells and to the sight of blood

CHAPTER 18: MAKE THE READER CARE

In this chapter, you'll learn psychological tricks to make the readers root for your protagonist.

PURPOSE

Why are they fighting? To involve your readers, give your fighters very strong reasons to fight. The stronger, the better. Make this purpose very clear before the fight starts, perhaps in a dialogue between the two opponents.

Examples for reasons for fighting
* to disarm the sentries
* to get out of the dungeon
* to do his job as a bodyguard
* to do his duty as a soldier of the king
* to free the princess
* to rescue his wife
* to punish the dissenters
* to defend his honour
* to show he won't be insulted
* to kill disbelievers
* to avenge his murdered father

MOTIVATION

Why is this so reason so important to them? The more important the motivation, the more exciting the scene. What would be the devastating consequences if he did not fight? The more devastating, the better.

Examples for devastating consequences

* If he doesn't disarm the sentries, he can't get into the fortress

* If he doesn't get out of the dungeon, he'll be executed

* If he doesn't do his job as a bodyguard, he'll get fired, be unemployed, and unable to feed his family

* If he doesn't do his duty as a soldier of the king, he'll be shot as a deserter

* If he doesn't free the queen, the monarchy will collapse

* If he doesn't rescue his wife, she'll be murdered

* If he doesn't punish the dissenters, there'll be a revolution

* If he doesn't defend his honour, his lady love will not respect him

* If he doesn't show he won't be insulted, the gang won't accept him as a leader

* If he doesn't kill disbelievers, he won't get a place in his religion's paradise

* If he doesn't avenge his murdered father, he will be ashamed for the rest of his life

There may be more than one devastating consequence of not fighting.

Purpose and motivation often overlap. It's no problem if they are not separate.

RAISING THE STAKES

To raise the stakes, make it important that he not only fights, but wins. What would be the devastating consequences of not winning?

Sometimes, they are the same consequences as for not fighting. Sometimes, they are different.

If the purpose is 'to do his duty for his king', the motivation for fighting is 'to avoid being shot as a deserter', and the motivation for winning is 'to survive the battle'.

Often, the devastating consequence of not winning is - death!

There may be more than one devastating consequence of losing the fight.

Just before the Climax of the fight, when all seems lost, and the hero is close to giving up, he remembers his purpose, and the devastating consequence of losing, and rallies his last strength.

EMOTION

A fight scene needs as much emotion as a love scene. The emotions are different, but just as strong.

What does the point of view character feel? What is the main emotion? Someone who feels 'fury' fights aggressively and rashly, while someone whose main emotion is 'fear' has a more defensive and cautious fighting style.

Emotions to choose from

* Fear - Anxiety - Panic - Terror (these four are similar but different)

* Anger - Fury - Outrage (these three are similar but different)

* Worry (e.g. about the injured hostage)

* Pride (in his own skill) - Contempt (for his unskilled cowardly opponent) - Confidence (these three are similar but different)

* Pity (for the enemy he has to kill)

* Religious fervour (often to the point of fanaticism)

* Shock - Surprise - Disbelief (these three are similar but different)

* Despair (when he thinks he's losing)

Each fighter probably feels several emotions during the fight scene, either at the same time, or one after the other. For example: at first, he feels contempt for his clumsy opponent. When he realises that his opponent is better than he thought, he feels surprise and shock. Then he realises that he may lose the fight, and feels panic. Then he remembers that his god wants him to kill the infidel, and he feels religious fervour.

You can spell out the point-of-view character's motivations and emotions. For the opponent, you may need to imply them.

STACKING THE ODDS

In a fight scene, readers always root for the disadvantaged fighter. The more heavily you stack the odds against your hero, the more the readers will root for him. It will also make the fight more exciting.

Think of one of the most famous fights of all times: David vs Goliath.

Goliath: a grown man, a giant, a professional warrior with fight experience, heavily armoured, superbly armed.

David: a boy, small, shepherd, without fight experience against humans, without armour, armed with a primitive weapon.

Readers have loved this scene for thousands of years because the odds are so heavily stacked against the hero. Can you do the same for your fight scene?

Stacking the odds against the hero is especially important for the final showdown between the hero and the villain near the end of the book. For this scene, really pile on the disadvantages. In earlier fight scenes, the odds can be more evenly stacked.

Here are some ideas for advantages for your antagonist (villain)

better weapon
mastery of the weapon
preparedness (anticipates the fight)
familiarity with terrain
greater number of fighters
surprise
ruthlessness (can fight dirty)
superior strength
superior stamina
superior stature
fighting experience

Here are some ideas for disadvantages for the protagonist (hero)

small stature

female
inexperienced
no weapon or inferior weapon
no armour or inferior armour
weakened, illness or starvation
exhausted
injured
unprepared
untrained
unfamiliar with terrain
restricted by code of honour (can't fight dirty)
few fighters (or he's alone)

To keep the scene plausible, your good guy should have some advantages, such as skill (even David had stone-slinging practice on his side). However, the bad guy should always have more advantages.

MANIPULATE THE READERS' INSTINCTS

The readers instinctively root for the female against the male, and for the defender against the attacker.

If your male hero fights against a female, the readers will be uncomfortable. If he's the attacker, and if he hurts the woman, the readers may even hate him, even if he does it for a noble cause. (By contrast, most readers enjoy reading about a woman who kicks male butt, and they don't mind in the least if she hurts him).

To make the readers root for the right person (for the attacker against the defender, or for the male against the female), you need to manipulate their sympathies. Do this by stacking the odds: The male attacker is exhausted and bleeding from many wounds and has lost his weapons, and his clothes are in tatters. His female opponent is a highly trained fighter, renowned for her ruthlessness, who wears state-of-the-art armour, carries a machine gun, and is accompanied by two Rottweiler dogs who are trained to kill. Now the reader will root for the man.

BLUNDERS TO AVOID

* Nothing at stake.... as if the characters put their lives at risk without purpose

* Absence of emotion... as if the fighter didn't feel fear, fury or despair

* Making it easy for the hero by giving him a superior weapon, superior armour, superior strength. and superior skills... as if he couldn't rise to a genuine challenge

CHAPTER 19: THE INSIDE EXPERIENCE

The best fight scenes are the ones where the reader forgets that it's only a story. How do you give the reader the feeling that he is actually fighting?

POINT OF VIEW

Fight scenes work best if they are presented from a single point of view. This allows the reader to identify with one fighter, and to experience all the excitement, thrill and triumph first hand.

In older novels, fight scenes were often written in omniscient point of view (a god-like perspective, seeing not only the Action, but what's going on in everyone's head and soul). Some of these omniscient fight scenes are excellent (for example in *The Three Musketeers* by Alexandre Dumas, 1844), but modern readers like to be inside one person at a time.

When writing for the modern market, I recommend choosing one point of view character for the fight, and sticking with it for the whole scene.

However, this depends on how you've handled PoV in the rest of your novel. If the whole novel is omniscient, then the fight scene should be omniscient as well. If you've frequently changed PoV in mid-scene, then you can change it in the middle of the fight scene, too. The best place for a PoV change is probably the Surprise.

If in doubt, stick to a single consistent PoV.

Showing motivation and emotion through PoV

In Chapter 18, you decided what motivates the fighters, and what they feel. How do you convey these elements to the reader?

I recommend spelling out the PoV's motivations. Spell it out twice (in different words): The first time in the Suspense section, the second time at the beginning of the Climax section when all seems lost.

Examples

He had to knock out the guard to get into the citadel.

If she lost this fight, her children would die.

This was his last chance to gain the jewel.

To show the PoV's emotions, use physical sensations as far as possible. Fight scenes are very physical, so try to describe how the emotions affect the body.

Examples

A hot wave of excitement surged through her veins.

Fear squeezed like an iron fist around his chest.

His stomach churned with acid fury.

Showing what goes on in the non-PoV character's mind is more difficult. You can't tell us what he thinks or feels without breaking PoV. However, you can imply a lot by showing his fighting style (a furious person fights aggressively and rashly, a frightened person fights defensively and evades a lot).

You may also be able to use dialogue to convey the opponent's motivation, probably in the Suspense section.

Examples

"On the king's orders, nobody may enter."

"At last, you're in my power. Now my brother's death will be avenged."

"The girl is mine. I will die before I give her up."

"The duke has promised a thousand pieces of gold for your dead body."

USING THE SENSES

To create an intense experience, use several senses. Don't rely exclusively on the sense of 'seeing', although it is an important sense.

When using the sense of 'seeing', show only what your PoV actually sees at that moment. During the fight, this is probably very little. The PoV sees his opponent's face, hands and weapon - and not much else. Don't show the sun sinking below the distant horizon, or the length of the river turning red with blood, or what the soldiers on the other side of the battlefield are doing, because the PoV can't see them. He simply doesn't have time to look at those things. Your PoV's full attention is on his opponent. If he allows himself to be distracted for even half a second, he's dead. In addition, the adrenaline in his bloodstream creates 'tunnel vision', so he couldn't see anything else even if he tried. You can use broader visual perspectives during the Suspense and Aftermath sections.

To create excitement in your fight scene, use the sense of 'hearing' a lot, especially the sound of weapons - zinging bullets, hissing arrows, clanking swords. In unarmed combat, you can use the panting breath, or the breaking of bones. In a real fight, the adrenaline can impair the sense of hearing, rendering even a thundering explosion as a faint whisper, and sometimes the fighter can hear nothing at all. However, this doesn't work well in fiction, because a good fight scene needs sounds. Another effect of the adrenaline rush is more useful: a roaring in the ears.

To create a sense of realism, use the sense of 'touching' now and then: describe how the weapon feels in the fighter's hand, what the ground feels like underfoot, and how it feels to be slammed against the wall. As the fight progresses, the adrenaline rush impairs the sense of touch, and the fighters may stumble or lose their grip on their weapon, although this is an effect which doesn't work well in most fiction scenes.

The sense of 'smelling' may not be active during the actual fight, but it can be used to great effect in the Aftermath section. If your PoV is an animal or a were, this sense may also play an important part during the Suspense, and there may be a strong reaction to the scent of any blood from fight injuries.

The sense of 'tasting' may not be appropriate, although you may describe the taste of blood in the mouth (which can happen when the fighter bites his tongue and also from internal injuries).

The sense of pain - if you regard it as a separate sense from 'touching' - is relevant in a fight scene. Fighting hurts. To create a sense of realism, mention pain at least once. You don't need to mention pain every time the PoV receives a blow - this would make him appear like a wuss - but two or three brief mentions are effective. You can keep these mentions very short, e.g. *Sharp pain zinged through his thigh.* The rush of adrenaline during the fight often blocks out some or all of the pain. In this case, the pain hits when the fight is over, in the Aftermath section.

Here's a section-by-section guide for inserting senses into your fight scene. Obviously, not every suggestion works for every fight scene. Leave out, add and change.

Suspense

Seeing - assessing terrain, useful for giving reader information. The opponent getting ready for the fight (male dominance posturing, subtle stretching of neck and back, licking lips.)

Hearing - background noises to create Suspense: owl hooting in the distance, a car door slamming out of sight, a wall clock ticking. Sounds of readying for the fight: Officer's commands, sound of loading gun.

Touching - how does the weapon feel in the hand: cold, smooth, heavy? Physical manifestations of emotions: Itching scalp, thudding heart, pressing bladder, dry throat, blood singing with excitement?

Start

Seeing - Totally focused on details of opponent's movements

Touching - Ground underfoot

Pain - first hit or blow

Action

Seeing - Opponent's face, hands, weapon, movements

Hearing - Sounds of weapons in action, e.g. zinging gunshots, clanking steel

Touching - The hand holding the weapon is slick with sweat or blood. Motor skills may get affected by adrenaline rush: stumbling, losing grip on weapon.

Surprise

Seeing - Possibly a wider view, taking in the Surprise event

Hearing - Announce the Surprise event with sounds

Climax

Seeing - Opponent's face, hands, weapons, movements

Hearing - Weapons

Touching - Blows jolting the body, getting slammed against the wall, hands chafing on the ground, fist in belly

Tasting - maybe taste of blood in mouth (it tastes coppery or metallic)

Aftermath

Seeing - Injuries, mutilated bodies, gore, contorted facial expressions, crows and vultures above the battlefield

Smelling - gunpowder, urine, blood, faeces, intestinal gasses

Pain - aching muscles and hurt from injuries as adrenaline wears off

BLUNDERS TO AVOID

* The character thinks deep philosophical thoughts... as if fighting off deadly blows were so easy that he could concentrate on something else

* While involved in close-up fighting, the PoV sees what happens some distance away (how his comrades are faring, how the sun sinks towards the horizon)... as if the fighting didn't require his full attention

* The POV experiences no pain during or after the fight

CHAPTER 20: ARMOUR

Warriors who expect a fight usually put on some kind of armour which shields them against bullets, cuts or blows.

TYPES OF ARMOUR

Even everyday clothing offers some slight protection: when fighting off a knife-wielding drug-crazed teenager, it's better to wear a jacket than to be naked, and a quilted winter coat or a motor-biker's thick leather jacket gives more than a thin cotton wrap.

People who expect armed combat put on the most protective clothing they own. If they fight frequently, they make or buy items which offer stronger protection.

Thick leather, especially when treated and strengthened, offers good (though not perfect) protection against arrows, swords and spears. Other basic historical armour includes glued-together layers of fabric, and thin wooden or bone platelets sewn onto cloth. In technologically advanced societies, wealthy people usually own metal armour.

Armour can be heavy, hot and uncomfortable to wear, and sometimes noisy, which makes it unsuitable for creeping up on an enemy undetected. After several hours in armour, the wearer may be tired and sweaty, and stink.

Every armour has gaps, because the wearer needs to see, breathe and move. The attacker tries to get at those spots, for example, eyes, armpits and groin.

Armour restricts mobility. A fighter who is encased from head to toe in metal cannot move well or fast, which is a disadvantage in a fight - especially when he tries to flee. On the other hand, armour which allows full range of movement leaves many vulnerable spots.

Designers of armour develop compromise solutions: armour which protects only the most important or vulnerable body parts (e.g. head, abdomen, sword arm, lower legs), or which moves with the wearer (for example the apron-like garment of leather strips guarding a Roman legionnaire's thighs and groin).

A cuirass is a breastplate, typically made from metal, protecting the wearer's heart and abdomen.

Greaves are shin guards, often made from metal or leather, usually strapped on, protecting the front of the lower legs in a sword fight.

Arm guards, sometimes called 'bracers', are also worn in sword fights, because each fighter will try to end the fight by severing his opponent's sword arm.

Helmets are the most important item of armour for historical fighters. Metal helmets offer the best protection but are heavy and expensive. Leather helmets are more frequent. Sometimes, leather or cloth caps are covered with pieces of metal, wood, bone or boar's tusks.

Most forms of armour are almost impossible to cut (slash, slice) through. However, thrusting (stabbing, piercing) can usually penetrate.

Modern armour usually involves a bulletproof vest (which may also be knife-proof) which protect the wearer's torso. It can be stiff and heavy, and the comfort level depends on whether the vest is made for the wearer's shape and size. These vests don't let the body breathe, which can lead to uncomfortable and stinking sweat, especially after prolonged wearing, after action, and in hot weather. The body armour can lose its effectiveness after several years, and you can create interesting plot situations if your protagonist is forced to wear a vest several years past its use-by date. If a shooter knows his opponent is wearing a bulletproof vest, he will avoid the chest and aim at the unprotected thighs or the head. State-of-the art body armour is far superior to that of some decades ago.

Armour is costly. Only a professional warrior is likely to possess good armour, and only kings and wealthy nobles can afford state-of-the art armour for the whole body. A conscripted peasant is lucky if he owns a leather cap.

Watch armour in action

http://www.youtube.com/watch?v=sEuhKRhrvRM&feature=related (medieval armour)

http://www.youtube.com/watch?v=GVcJP8YxmKE (testing bullet-proof vests)

http://www.youtube.com/watch?v=3RWeQuIduXA (ancient Roman armour)

SHIELDS

Shields are carried, rather than worn, and they don't impair the mobility so much. However, a fighter carrying a shield cannot use that hand for a weapon.

Typically, a fighter carries a sword or spear in one hand, a shield in the other. Large shields offer almost whole-body protection, and the fighter can even duck behind them, for example during a barrage of thrown spears, but they are cumbersome to carry and move. A small shield protects only a section of the body, and the fighter moves it rapidly to deflect each individual blow.

Shields often consist of wooden frames covered with leather, hides or metal. They are relatively cheap to make, so a war leader may have them mass-produced to equip his army, or individual fighters make or buy their own. Sometimes, shields are painted with heraldic emblems or with scary faces.

A shield can also be used as a formidable weapon, for example by ramming a shield under the opponent's chin or slamming it down on his feet.

Shields tend to block the wielder's vision. Modern riot police sometimes use shields of transparent plastic.

If your protagonist is a woman, the shield offers interesting opportunities, because it favours the smaller fighter. The same sized shield protects a larger area of a small person's body than a large person's. When the fighting gets very close, the smaller fighter is well-positioned to hit the shield into the opponent's face or jaw. To make this plausible, your heroine needs a strong arm, because shields are heavy.

Units of fighters may use shield formations, such as the tortoise of the Roman legions which serves to advance even in a rain of spears, arrows, rocks and fire, the shield walls of the Vikings, and the way the ancient Greek hoplites each shielded not himself but the man next to him.

Watch shields in action

http://www.youtube.com/watch?v=VMuSyEud3BE
(Roman testudo shield formation)

BLUNDERS TO AVOID

* Sword maidens in belly-baring 'come and gut me' costume

* Warriors going into battle with state-of-the-art swords - but no shields

CHAPTER 21: FIGHT SITUATIONS

BRAWL

Brawls are spontaneous fights. Typically, they break out among young men, often under the influence of alcohol, starting when one man accuses the other of something (e.g. cheating at cards). A brawl may be between two fighters, but other people may take sides and get involved.

Most brawls are unarmed, involving mostly 'striking' kind fight moves especially with the fists (see Chapter 11). Use the words 'punch', 'jab', 'box', 'smash', 'slam'. A brawl may escalate into an armed fight, either with improvised weapons such as beer bottles and chairs (see Chapter 9), or with knives (see Chapter 5).

Anger is the dominant emotion.

In the Suspense section, you can convey the PoV's anger with phrases such as

His stomach churned with hot fury.

His anger reached boiling point.

Show the other person's angry body language, for example:

His lips tightened and his chin rose.

He shook a meaty fist in the air.

DUEL

A duel is a fight between two people, with pre-agreed rules. Both parties agree to fight each other, and they agree to the rules, the location and the weapons. Sometimes, a duel is arranged on the spur of the moment; at other times, it may be arranged hours or days in advance.

Duels are almost always about matters of honour. The person who feels offended in their honour - or who considers his woman's or his family's honour insulted - demands 'satisfaction', that is, he challenges the other to a duel.

Refusing a challenge would brand a person as a coward. However, the person who has been challenged usually gets the right to choose the place, the time and the weapon, which gives him some advantage.

Duellists are usually young men from the upper classes. In some societies and historical periods, duelling was so epidemic that it was the most frequent cause of death among young men. Only members of the same social class duelled; it was considered dishonourable to duel someone of lower status, and low-ranking people didn't have the right to challenge their betters.

Duelling is usually armed combat, and any type of weapon is possible. The most frequently used weapons are stabbing swords (for fencing fights) and handguns, but the duellists might also fight with poisonous snakes, cricket bats, pitchforks, or any other usual or unusual arms.

Before the fight, the duellists agree on rules. In a society where duels are common, they may agree to follow the established rules. Otherwise, they create their own. Both combatants behave with utmost courtesy and consideration, even if they hate each other's guts.

A fight may be 'to the death' (the survivor wins) or 'first blood' (the duel is over when one of them is wounded; the uninjured fighter wins). If the duel is to the death, each may promise to support the other's widow and orphans.

If the duel is fought about matters of honour, the duel erases the dishonour. Whoever survives - whether one or both - is not supposed to bring the matter up again.

Readers like fair fighting in duel scenes, especially when the hero and the villain outdo each other with polite fairness.

Each duellist may invite an assistant, called a 'second'. The two seconds act as referees and as witnesses. They also carry messages, measure out the distance for the shooting, and check that everything is fair. You can create interesting plot situations if the duellists are scrupulously fair, but one of the seconds is cheating.

There may also be a doctor or healer, a referee or a judge present.

If the law forbids duelling, the victor may face a charge of murder. To prevent this, the duellists and their seconds may create a situation so precisely timed that the witnesses can testify that both duellists acted in simultaneous self-defence.

A duel scene may contain more dialogue than other fight scenes, especially in the Suspense section, when the fighters agree on the rules and each tries to be more polite than the other. The Climax section is important; flesh it out.

Here's a perfect duelling scene worth studying: **http://www.youtube.com/watch?v=SVaslN1NiT0** *(Rob Roy)*

AMBUSH

In this kind of fight, one party is prepared, the other unprepared. For example, a highwayman holding up a stage coach, or native rebels luring the invading army into a trap.

It can involve two people, or two groups, or whole armies.

The ambushers choose a time when their opponents are vulnerable (e.g. unarmed, distracted or drunk). They also pick the ideal location.

A highwayman chooses a steep section of the slope where the coach has to slow down and can neither turn around nor escape. The native rebels pick a spot when the invading soldiers march single-file through a narrow gorge, block their exit and throw rocks down at them. The ambushers always have the advantage.

This can even out the odds. In a carefully planned ambush, a pair of highwaymen can rob a coach with ten passengers, and a dozen poorly equipped native rebels can annihilate three hundred superbly armed soldiers.

When writing the scene from the point of view of the ambusher, the Suspense section is long. When writing it from the point of view of the ambushed party, it may be as short as a single sentence.

ASSASSINATION

This is a murder, carried out quickly, quietly and efficiently, usually by professional killers (assassins), sometimes for political reasons.

Weapons favoured by assassins

* The garrotte: a string for quiet strangling, often in the victim's own home

* The stabbing dagger: useful for killing someone quickly and quietly in a crowd, for example by driving the dagger from below the chest up into the heart

* The rifle: shooting from a distance

Most assassins pride themselves in not hurting bystanders.

If the assassination succeeds, it happens so fast, the victim is dead before he realises what is happening. This barely deserves to be called a fight.

However, a failed assassination attempt can lead to an interesting fight scene. The intended victim spots the attacker just one heartbeat before he strikes. If the victim is the PoV, you can make this dramatic by letting him sense a change in the environment, perhaps a faint sound that shouldn't be there such as a rustling in the twigs behind him, or an almost inaudible creak in a floorboard. Or perhaps he catches a flicker of movement reflected in the shiny metal handrail, or sees a shifting shadow. Sometimes another character spots the danger and shouts out a warning just in time.

Since assassins are highly skilled professionals who choose the perfect location and situation and operate with stealth, the victim has to have sharp senses and extremely fast reactions. He has a fraction of a second to spin around and leap away. He needs to be even faster to catch the assassin and involve him in a fight, because assassins are masters at escape.

If the scene is from the assassin's point of view, the Suspense section is probably long. If it is from the target's point of view, it is very short, perhaps as little as half a sentence, because it is unexpected and happens fast.

RIOT

A riot is a large-scale fight which starts spontaneously. It originates from intense emotions such as outrage and hatred, often based on political, racial, or religious fervour, and quickly turns to violence. Typically, it breaks out in a place where people crowd together and emotions run high, for example, in a football stadium, at a protest rally, or at the funeral of a public figure. Soon, it spills over, and it may spread across a town or a whole country, and last for days.

During the Suspense section, your protagonist may sense emotions boiling up around her, she may hear angry yells and shouted slogans, or see violent fighting some distance away. She may get caught up in it suddenly; this is the Start section.

Rioters often use improvised weapons (see Chapter 9) or knives (Chapter 5).

People who get swept up in the events are typically bare-headed, while intentional rioters often wear hoods, scarves covering their faces, or even masks. When police or soldiers try to contain the violence, they are met with hatred. Rioters are not amenable to reasoning.

During riots, there is often vandalism, and you can create a realistic atmosphere by describing the sounds of shattering glass and the acrid smell of smoke.

CHAPTER 22: GROUP VS GROUP, ONE VS MANY

Group fights, and a single fighter taking on a crowd, pose special challenges for the writer.

ONE GROUP AGAINST ANOTHER

When a group of people fights against another group of people, make sure there are more bad guys than good guys, to engage the readers' sympathies.

Give each group a sense of identity. In real life, groups fighting against other groups bolster their spirit creating a mental 'us versus them' divide. This makes it easier to feel as a team, and to fight the 'others'. Sometimes, this is a microcosm of racial, religious, or social conflict. Here are some ideas: mods versus rockers, punks versus yuppies, skateboarders versus rollerbladers, students from School A versus students from School B, long-time residents versus immigrants, blacks versus whites, Christians versus heathens, Asians versus Hispanics, the Smiths versus the Joneses, cat lovers versus dog lovers, old money versus nouveau riche, people from this side of the river versus those from the opposite shore, rebels versus establishment, werewolves versus vampires, humans versus paranormals, earthlings versus aliens.

The clearer the division, the more motivated the fighters are to beat the 'others'. It also makes it easier for the reader to follow the action. In the movies, this is often emphasised with different costuming: guys with white hats versus guys with black hats, guys with blue capes versus guys with red capes. In the absence of such easy visual clues, you need to create word pictures which differentiate the two groups in other ways. Perhaps they dress differently, have different weapons, or use different languages or speech patterns.

When a group of people get involved in a fight, one of them is the leader who makes the decisions and to whom the others look for instruction. This may be the established leader - such as the captain of that team, the head girl of that school, the oldest of the siblings - or someone who has the respect of the others and takes charge spontaneously when the situation arises.

Group fights are easiest to write in omniscient point of view. Many of literature's great fight scenes are in omniscient PoV (e.g. the three musketeers and d'Artagnan against five of the cardinal's henchmen in *The Three Musketeers* by Alexandre Dumas). However, unless the whole novel is in omniscient, it's not a good idea for your fight scene.

Choose the point-of-view character who is involved in most action, and show only what he can see. Avoid sentences like *Meanwhile, at the other end of the bridge...* because that's either omniscient or head-hopping, and *From the corner of the eye, he observed...* because he won't be able to observe anything. Perhaps you can create a break in the fight during which the PoV can briefly glimpse how his comrades are doing. For example, he has just killed one bad guy and has two seconds before the next one comes at him.

If the plot demands more than one point of view for the scene, choose a natural break, probably during the Surprise section.

ONE AGAINST A GROUP

Scenes in which one fighter defeats several opponents with his sword or his bare hands can be fun, but are hardly plausible. They are probably 'entertaining' fight scenes. Here are several ideas how to create an illusion of reality for such a scene.

How can one hero fight several people at once?

* Keep the number of opponents realistic: two or three, not twenty or thirty.

* He is more highly trained than all his opponents. A martial arts master can take out three or four untrained attackers.

* He chooses a position where his opponents can come only from one direction, so he has to fight only in one direction. For example, if he stands on top of a tower, he needs to fight only downwards. However, this can backfire, because if the opponents gain the upper hand, he can't escape. A place where the opponents come from one direction but he has an escape route is better: at the end of a corridor through which the enemies must come, at the end of a narrow bridge they must cross. This leaves the question of where the bodies go. Unless he can toss them down a ravine, they are going to pile up between him and the gang.

* He identifies the group's leader, and takes him out first. Once their leader is down, the others will lose confidence, and either give up or fight with reduced courage.

* He may hit them while they're spread out, unable to communicate with each other. This way, he only needs to fight one or two at a time. He may even create a situation in which forces them to spread out.

* If several attackers back him against a wall, and he can move neither forward nor back, he can still move laterally, sliding along the wall. This allows him to get off-centre of the group, and either escape or fight the guy at the outer edge.

* He uses a weapon which can take out several opponents in a short time. With a machine gun, it's easy to mow down a dozen people. However, readers don't like heroes who do this, even in self-defence.

Why are they so daft?

In many movie fight scenes, a dozen or more bad guys gang up on the hero. But instead of attacking him all at once, they take their turns fighting him one-to-one, which allows him to take out one after the other. This is highly implausible: real life bad guys are not so daft.

If you want to write a scene in which the bad guys wait their turn to be individually defeated, consider giving it at least a token of plausibility. Here are some ideas.

* The hero has taken up position in a place where only one person can access him at a time.

* Since only four or five can surround him at a time, the others have to stand back.

* The attackers don't arrive simultaneously. They come running, and each attacks the hero as soon as he gets there.

* The gang has a code of honour which demands one-to-one fights. If so, establish this code earlier in the book.

* The fight is an initiation ritual for new gang members. To be accepted as a full member, the recruit must kill a man in a one-to-one fight. The established members stand back as each recruit takes his turn attempting to pass the test.

Reader sympathy

Fights in which one hero takes out several opponents can make it difficult to maintain reader sympathy. On the one hand, readers always root for the smaller party, and one person attacked by many gains their goodwill. But if he succeeds, the reader's sympathy may turn to horror or contempt.

* If he uses a weapon against unarmed opponents, or a superior weapon against poorly armed ones, readers will view him as a butcher. The scene can be boring as well as gruesome, and the reader's sympathies may be lost forever.

* If he takes out many opponents at once, readers don't believe that he really had to fight. They conclude that he possesses some kind of superpower which guarantees victory, and that makes the fight scene uninteresting.

* If the novel contains more than one scene in which the hero defeats several opponents, the readers will view him as a mass murderer. They'll be disgusted and bored by the piled-up corpses.

It's probably best to avoid one-against-many scenes, except at the novel's climax. If the book has only one such scene, and it comes near the end, the scene can be exciting. Keep the number of opponents realistic. Arrange it so that the hero fights the henchmen first, and the showdown between hero and villain comes last, to keep the tension high. (See Chapter 28).

Here are clips with ideas how to make a one-versus-many fight realistic:

http://www.youtube.com/watch?v=Zp-EV8Q7VIY

http://www.youtube.com/watch?v=8EewcuZ3LBw&feature=related

http://www.youtube.com/watch?v=DieOiJerm8s&feature=related

BLUNDERS TO AVOID

* Pitching a large number of good guys against a small number of bad guys. (The reader will root for the bad guys)

* Gang members waiting to take turns to fight the hero one-to-one. (If they have sense, several will attack him at once)

* Hero easily dispatching large numbers of enemies at once

CHAPTER 23: BATTLE

Battles, with their large-scale carnage, lend themselves more to 'gritty' than to 'entertaining'. However, literature often requires 'entertaining' battle scenes, especially in heroic fantasy fiction.

In some famous works of literature, pairs of fighters are somehow isolated from the masses and fight it out in one-to-one combat. The battle scenes at Troy in Homer's *Iliad* are an example. Maybe you can do this in your novel, too. Perhaps everyone else has already fallen, with just one man standing on each side.

Point of view is difficult to handle, unless you're writing omniscient. The individual fighter can't see what goes on a few feet from him, let alone what's happening at the other end of the battlefield or how the sun dyes the horizon bloody red.

Stack the odds against your heroes. The readers' natural sympathies lie with the smaller army. The greater you can make the numerical difference, the better. The evil overlord's army is bigger than the hero's, and it is much better equipped, too.

Have you heard of the battle of Thermopylae (480 BC), when three hundred Spartans defended Greece against thousands of invading Persians? The Spartans knew they were going to die, and fought anyway, to gain time for their homeland to prepare further defence.

Since then, thousands of battles have been fought - and forgotten. Thermopylae is remembered. The story has been retold in many novels, non-fiction books, and films. The incredible bravery against overwhelming odds still rouses audiences' emotions. When writing your own battle scenes, use Thermopylae as your inspiration.

Battles don't just happen: they are planned. At least one side seeks the battle and is prepared. While there have been occasions in history when enemy units bumped into each other by accident and started fighting, this is not the norm, and unless you're very knowledgeable about military matters, it won't come across as plausible.

The generals plan a battle strategy in advance, and make sure that their officers know it. In the heat of the battle, it's often impossible to change strategy or give orders. Sometimes, soldiers are still fighting when the battle has already been decided, because they don't know that their king is dead or the enemy general has surrendered.

Often, the location decides the outcome of the battle. Generals choose the location carefully - and so should you, the author!

If the battle takes place on a slope, the army uphill has a huge advantage, because it's easier to fight downhill than uphill, and because missiles fly further.

Each general tries to make the battle happen in terrain which favours his own army, and where the enemy can't fully deploy his.

For example, chariots are fearsome on the plain, but useless in the mountains. Foot archers can fight on any terrain, especially in the mountains. The general who has many chariots will try to force a battle on the plain, while the general who has archers will try to lure his enemy into mountainous terrain.

If one general has a small army and his enemy has a large one, he'll try to lure them into a gorge or other restricted space where they can't move.

Armies are organised in units either by level of skill and experience (elite, veterans, novices, untrained peasants...) or by weapons and equipment (cavalry, infantry, archers, spearmen, chariots...) or both.

Before the battle, the general probably addresses the troops, firing their fighting spirit and courage.

This pep talk may include depersonalising the enemy, because soldiers are more willing to kill monsters than to kill fellow human beings. It's easy to kill a man whom you consider a menace to your children, and difficult to kill him if you think of him as a fellow human who loves his children as much as you love yours.

Noble thoughts and ideals have no room during battle. The thinker of noble thoughts and carrier of high ideals during battle won't survive. If you want to show your hero's nobility, do it when the fighting is over in the Aftermath section (for example, in the treatment of surviving enemies).

Consider using unusual, interesting or extreme weather to make your battle scene unusual. Imagine pristine snow which gets trampled, becomes slippery, and stains red with blood. Or a strong wind which blows arrows off course. Or blistering heat and glaring sun. Or week-long rain turning the field into knee-deep mud, making it difficult for foot soldiers, let alone horses or chariots. Or fog blocking the view of the enemy.

When writing a battle scene, you can use the same six-part structure as for a one-to-one fight.

Use the Suspense section to describe the terrain, and to convey the battle strategy.

During the Start section, both armies shoot missiles to take out as many of the enemy as possible before they get close. In a historical novel, clouds of arrows may darken the sky before the battle begins.

For the Action remember to keep to your chosen point of view: The warrior sees only what's immediately before him. He won't be able to assess how the overall battle is progressing.

Although real battles and 'gritty' battle scenes seldom have a Surprise, you may like to create one for an 'entertaining' scene, especially if it's near the end of the novel. Perhaps a relief force arrives to support one army, or a sudden downpour turns the ground into mud.

Writing the Climax section can be difficult because the individual warrior is probably not aware of the Climax of the battle. If possible, arrange it so your hero kills an important enemy personage, maybe the general. This may not reflect the reality of most battles, but it pleases the readers.

The Aftermath section is important in a battle scene. This is where you can inject realism. In a 'gritty' battle scene, the Aftermath section is long, detailed, shocking and gory. In the 'entertaining' style it's short, because you don't want to disgust readers with the realities of war. If you're aiming for something in between, I recommend writing about a paragraph describing the battlefield, perhaps leaving out the most gruesome parts.

Soon after the battle, there'll be carrion birds (e.g. crows, vultures) feeding on the corpses. There'll be humans (probably the victorious soldiers) gathering up reusable weapons (because weapons are valuable) and looting the corpses. The battlefield is covered in blood, gore, and amputated limbs. The stench is awful, because in death, the bladder and bowels have opened. Plus, there's the smell from injuries, not just blood (which starts to stink only after a while) but the content of stomachs and intestines from belly wounds. The stench gets worse after a few hours, especially if the weather is hot. After some hours, the corpses will be crawling with flies, and before long, there'll be maggots.

BLUNDERS TO AVOID

* Battles breaking out spontaneously without planning or preparation by anyone

* Archers shooting arrows after the close-up fighting has started

* The soldier observes what his mates are doing at the other side of the battlefield and how the sun sets on the horizon... as if the immediate danger didn't require all his attention

*The soldier is aware of the overall development of the battle while he's involved in the fighting... as if he had a means to know

CHAPTER 24: SIEGE WARFARE

In a siege, the readers' natural sympathies lie with the defenders. If the PoV fights on the side of the attackers, you may need to manipulate the reader. Give the defenders state-of-the-art defence technology, and let them commit some atrocious deeds, such as killing an envoy and tossing his mutilated body over the wall.

There are two types of siege: 'active' and 'passive'.

ACTIVE SIEGE

In an active siege, the besiegers use force to get in. They attack the walls with cannons, catapults and battering rams. They use long ladders to climb the walks. They may build a ramp to reach the top of the walls (this takes months), or dig a tunnel to make part of the wall collapse.

The defenders hurl missiles at the attackers: arrows, stones, hot oil, burning pitch. They try to set the battering rams on fire.

Women, children and old people - who are normally non-combatants in other forms of warfare - play an active role in the defence during an active siege. They take their turns hurling stones and pouring boiling oil on the enemy.

If your PoV is inside the castle/fortress/citadel, you can create enormous Suspense: will the wall/the gate hold? Describe the sounds of the battering rams/cannons /catapults against the walls/gates.

The outcome of an active siege often depends on state-of-the-art technology: What is better - the siege machinery or the defence structures? It also depends on the defenders' preparedness: Have they strengthened their walls, or have they let the ancient walls fall into disrepair? Do they have enough stones/arrows/oil?

http://www.youtube.com/watch?v=SAW2LxJRLqM (*The Lord of the Rings*)

PASSIVE SIEGE

In the passive siege, the besiegers cut off the defenders' contact with the outside world. With no supplies getting in, the aim is to starve the defenders into submission. This is quite boring for the attackers, who sit and watch day after day. The word 'siege' comes from the Latin word 'sedere' and the French 'siéger', which both mean 'sit'.

A passive siege typically lasts several months. It ends either when the besiegers run out of patience, or when the defenders give up. Typically, this is because of one of these three factors: hunger (stocks of food are depleted), thirst (empty cisterns), treachery (someone who doesn't like starving opens the gate).

Inside the besieged town, castle, citadel or fortress, the situation is grim. The place is crowded with refugees fleeing from the marauding army. There may be ten times as many people inside the citadel than normally. And there's usually not much food. Even with rationing, food soon runs short. Water may also be sparse. Most castles have a well inside the town. If this doesn't yield enough water for everyone, or if there is no well, the defenders won't stand a chance. With so many people cramped into limited space for a short time, and the stress of being under siege, and the fear of their fate, tempers run short, and there's a lot of aggression and blaming. In the crowded conditions, infectious diseases spread, and epidemics may wipe out a large portion of the population.

During a passive siege, the besiegers also have problems with supplies. They scavenge the surrounding countryside, but there probably isn't enough food to supply a whole army.

Siege warfare is costly. During a passive siege, the soldiers need to be provisioned, even if they don't fight. The ruler may well decide that it's not worth the expense.

If an army sets out to conquer a land, they may offer lenient terms to any town which surrenders immediately. They may spare the town and its population, and simply appoint their own governor there. This leniency tempts many towns into instant surrender, which makes the conquest quick, easy and cost-effective.

Any town which puts up a resistance gets punished cruelly, to set an example to other towns. The survivors will be raped, impaled, tortured, burnt alive, sold into slavery. This harsh treatment scares other towns into submitting.

Use the weather to make the situation even more uncomfortable for either side, e.g. blistering heat, freezing hold, monsoon downpour.

The Aftermath of a passive siege may involve a lot of corpses inside (either from starvation and sickness, or from mass executions). On the outside, the surrounding land may be impoverished because of plunder and confiscation, and settlements may be vandalised.

A passive siege is a structural challenge for the novelist, because it goes on for weeks or months, sometimes even years, so it may be the background of several scenes rather than the focus of one scene.

COMBINED ACTIVE/PASSIVE SIEGE

A siege can be a combination of active and passive. For example, the attackers may try to batter the walls down, find that the walls won't yield, and settle down to cut off the supplies. Or they may embark on a passive siege, but at the same time build a ramp leading up to the citadel's walls (as the Romans did at Masada).

CHAPTER 25: NAUTICAL FIGHTS

This chapter will help you add authenticity to your scene and avoid embarrassing blunders.

WHAT ARE THEY FIGHTING FOR?

In a fight between two ships, each captain has one of these three goals:

1. Sink the other ship

Methods: ram, set on fire, or blow a hole in the hull

Typical contexts: out-and-out warfare, especially in the ancient Mediterranean

Advantages: fast, no person-to-person fighting

Drawbacks: getting close enough to the other ship exposes own ship, mass murder of the crew, no chance to get their cargo and provisions

2. Plunder the other ship

Methods: disable the ship (by damaging mast, oars, and other means of propulsion and steering), board the ship, get cargo and provisions, kill crew (optional), sink ship

Typical context: piracy, privateering (pirate and adventure fiction)

Advantages: valuable cargo can be sold for profit, much-needed drinking water and food sustain own crew for a while longer, selected captives can be ransomed or sold as slaves

Drawbacks: dangerous, need to get enough to gain access to ship, crew unlikely to surrender, ferocious fighting, great risk to own men

3. Capture the other ship

Methods: capture ship without damaging it significantly, keep enemy crew alive, put own officers in charge of enemy crew, add enemy ship to own fleet or collect prize money from the government (the ship will then get a new flag, get renamed and refitted)

Typical context: 18th and 19th century Europe (including Regency romances)

Advantages: minimal loss of life, humane, gaining a ship (ships are extremely valuable), chance to get rich quick means highly motivated crew (members of the winning crew gets a share of the prize money which can be enough to set them up for life)

Disadvantages: difficult to capture a ship without first damaging it, captains may take foolish risks in the hope of prize money, captive crew needs feeding, captive crew may mutiny

WEAPONS

You need to consider two groups of weapons:

The ship's weapons

The ship may be equipped to attack, or to repel attacks from, another ship.

It may have a ram at the bow (that's the front of the ship), suitable for driving into the hull of an enemy ship. To do this, the captain needs to manoeuvre the ship so its front faces the enemy vessel's vulnerable side. Naturally, the enemy captain will try to do the same. There's also the danger that his own vessel gets stuck in the enemy's hull, and they go down together.

Artillery allows attacks from a distance. The Byzantines hurled 'Greek fire' at enemy ships to set them aflame. Especially in the 18th and 19th centuries, warships (and many trading vessels) carried cannons. When using artillery, the ship with the latest technology (able to inflict the greater damage at greater speed and from the greater distance) has the advantage.

Individual's weapons

Sailors, especially in historical novels, may carry knives. These are multi-purpose tools and weapons. For suggestions on how to write a knife fight, see Chapter 5.

The swords used by mariners, sailors and pirates were almost always slashing swords (for cutting, slashing and slicing, very sharp, with a lightly curving blade). For suggestions how to write a fight with slashing swords, see Chapter 3. The types of sword most associated with fighting at sea are cutlasses. These videos demonstrate the use of cutlasses:

http://www.youtube.com/watch?v=kVhV8ENwIBY

http://www.youtube.com/watch?v=R-qpedUbxBc

http://www.youtube.com/watch?v=6EelCMaWW6Y

SHIP OR BOAT?

The worst blunder a writer can commit is using the word 'boat' when writing about a 'ship', and vice versa. It's easy to confuse the two terms, because the distinctions are blurred, and they changed throughout history. When deciding whether it's a ship or a boat, consider the following factors:

- The historical period. (Different periods used different definitions.)

- The vessel's size. (A ship is usually bigger. A ship can carry a boat; a boat cannot carry a ship.)

- The vessel's weight. (Ships are heavier than boats.)

- The purpose. (Fishing vessels, ferries and submarines are typically boats, regardless of size.)

- The number of masts. (With three or more masts, it's a ship.)

- The number of decks. (With more than one deck, it's a ship.)

- The shape. (A flat bottom usually means it's a boat.)

- Where most activity takes place. (If on deck, it's a boat; if below decks, it's a ship.)

- Where the vessel travels. (If on a river, it's probably a boat; if on an ocean, it's probably a ship.)

Make sure you use the term the crew of that type of vessel use themselves, especially when the PoV of the scene is the vessel's captain.

To avoid using the word 'ship' (or 'boat') fifty times in a scene, don't be tempted to replace 'ship' with 'boat' or vice versa, because they aren't synonyms. You can use the word 'vessel', and you can also use a word which defines the built or function: the ferry, the schooner, the brigantine, the cutter, the cruiser, the ferry etc.

PROPULSION AND STEERING

Another embarrassing blunder is to use a ship like a car, stopping, starting, swerving and reversing rapidly. A ship - especially a historical vessel - can do these things only slowly, under certain circumstances, if at all.

It depends on the means by which it is propelled.

Wind power (sailing) creates high speed, enables long distances, and doesn't require the vessel to carry fuel. However, it limits the directions in which the vessel can move, and in the absence of wind, no movement is possible. Wind-dependent vessels can't carry out speedy manoeuvres in a battle. Felling the mast will cripple the vessel and prevent its escape, perfect for plundering.

Oars (rowing) allow for greater manoeuvrability, rapid direction changes, and relatively quick starts and stops. However, rowing doesn't achieve great speed and isn't suitable for long distances. Some vessels, for example those of ancient Greece, have dozens of oars arranged in tiers, which increases the speed, but men busy rowing aren't available to fight in the battle. Often, sailing vessels have oars, combining the advantages of both methods.

Steam can create speed and doesn't depend on wind. However, it requires carrying coal, which limits the amount of cargo the ship can carry, and how far it can travel without refuelling. Some steamers have supplementary sails, so they save energy when the wind is favourable.

Vessels fuelled with oil or nuclear power can travel vaster distances, and fast. However, they still can't stop, start, swerve and reverse as quickly as a motorcar.

SPACE

The deck of a ship or boat makes an interesting location for a fight scene. The space is limited (fighters can fall overboard) and three-dimensional (fighters can climb up a mast, jump down, or leap onto another deck). It may also be full of obstacles: as well as the masts, there may be coiled ropes and possibly clutter, particularly if the crew is undisciplined and the captain disorganised. There may be crates and barrels of cargo and provisions; although those are normally stored in the hold, the vessel may be carrying more cargo than it has room in the hold, for example, if it's a pirate ship which has just plundered another vessel. There may even be livestock, such as chickens in cages and goats tethered to the mast, intended to provide fresh meat on the long voyage.

Vessels may roll, sway and tilt, especially small vessels in windy weather, and this can add interesting effects to your fight scene.

ATMOSPHERE

A sea battle or shipboard fight offers great scope for interesting sounds which make the scene exciting, for instance roaring cannons, crashing masts, splintering wood, panicked chickens, waves crashing against the hull, the wind whipping the sails, the splashing of men overboard.

BLUNDERS TO AVOID

* Blasting a hole in a ship's hull, and then boarding it

* Vessels which can be stopped, started and steered as easily as cars

* Calling a ship a boat and vice versa

CHAPTER 26: GENRES

Different genres require different treatment of fight scenes. Here are some suggestions.

ROMANCE

Romance readers want to be caressed and wooed, not shocked or disgusted, so the fight scenes are always entertaining. However, romance readers want to believe that the fights could be real, so you need to create an illusion of reality.

Avoid the excesses of entertaining scenes - the theatricality, the fancy acrobatics, the implausible feats - and add some gritty elements to create realism: mention how the ground feels underfoot, use spatial restrictions, show the effect of the weather, describe sounds and smells.

To avoid grossing your readers out, use little pain, very little blood, and no gore. Minor wounds are acceptable, and you can use them to further the couple's relationship. If one of them gets injured, the other may clean and bandage the wound in the Aftermath section, which may be an opportunity for touching and tender care.

If you're looking to add a layer of erotic tension to the fight, you will find ideas in Chapter 27.

Fight scenes in romance tend to be short, seldom stretching over more than seven hundred words. Most are much shorter.

Sub-genres with a strong Action component, such as paranormal or futuristic romance, often contain several fight scenes: in the first, the hero comes to the heroine's rescue; in the second, she may rescue him; in the final scene they fight side by side against the villain and his sidekicks.

HUMOUR

In humour, fights don't have much reality, and they may parody serious fight scenes. To make it funny, combine elements of the expected (what has been done so much in fight scenes that it has become a cliché) with elements of the unexpected (new twists). Contrast totally entertaining elements with totally gritty ones for good effect. The grit can be so over-the-top that the reader doesn't take it seriously.

Here is a famous example which contrasts over-the-top entertaining facets (e.g. much dialogue) with over-the-top gritty ones (e.g. unsurvivable injuries), and expected tropes (e.g. clichéd dialogue) with unexpected twists.

http://www.youtube.com/watch?v=gXY9TuuwyL8 (*Monty Python and the Holy Grail*)

FANTASY

Fight scenes in fantasy tend to be entertaining, but often with a considerable amount of grit. Since a novel's plot requires the reader to suspend their disbelief about dragons, unicorns, magicians and enchanted treasures, it helps if other aspects of the novel - such as the fights - are realistic.

Fantasy readers love heroes who are unusually skilled fighters, especially with weapons. The hero usually excels at using one type of weapon (often a sword), and he may have a special relationship with it. For skills, see Chapter 13. For swords, see Chapter 4.

Readers enjoy a weapons duel between the hero and an equally skilled opponent. The Climax section of the scene is detailed.

If the fight involves magic, use the tips in Chapter 10.

SCIENCE FICTION

Fights in Science fiction are almost always armed.

Science fiction readers love creative innovations, so don't just copy a weapon from a Sci-Fi movie – light sabres are boring - , but invent one for your book. To make it plausible, take a real weapon which is in use today - say, a handgun -, and extrapolate: how might sophisticated technology improve on it?

Perhaps the weapon will be more accurate, or have more firepower, or reach farther. Perhaps the level of power is adjustable. Maybe the weapon is voice-activated, or changes colour as it self-camouflages to adapt to the environment.

To make the fight interesting, the weapon needs a flaw or limitation. Perhaps it doesn't function well in the different gravity of a certain planet. Or maybe it works with solar energy, the battery is about to run out, and there's no sun for recharging. Maybe it's so sophisticated that only highly trained users can operate it. Or perhaps it requires the owner's password, so as to render it useless to the enemy - which means the fallen man's comrades won't be able to use it either.

HORROR

Fights in horror novels are mostly gritty. Readers aren't put off by violence, gore or death, as long as these are plot relevant. Gore for gore's sake doesn't work. The Suspense and Aftermath sections may both be long, and the Surprise section may contain a cruel twist.

The scene may contain some entertaining elements, for example, the fight may last longer than it does in reality, but grit prevails.

THRILLER

Fight scenes in thrillers are very gritty, depicting real pain and real violence, even gory violence. There may be severe injuries and deaths. However, they also include entertaining elements, such as long duration and the hero showing off his skill.

The Climax of the thriller typically involves a showdown between the hero and the villain. This is an intense, prolonged fight, usually in a dangerous location such as a burning house or a sinking ship.

The Suspense section is long.

The protagonist often has advanced-level training in unarmed combat, in shooting, and in fight strategy.

COSY MYSTERY

Unlike the thriller, the cosy mystery avoids violence. Most fighting, including the murders, takes place off-stage. Fights are very short, typically just a couple of paragraphs within another scene.

HISTORICAL

Fight scenes in historical novels may be gritty or entertaining or anything in between.

When writing armed fights, make sure that the weapon was available in that period. A gun fired before it has been invented can ruin the plausibility of the whole book.

However, it is plausible that a character owns a weapon from a different culture, because weapons were traded over vast distances, and carried away by battle victors.

Poor people had poor weapons - if any. Only wealthy nobles could afford state-of-the art arms and armour. Peasants had to make do with farm implements and wooden sticks. You can create interesting plot situations if your character needs a sword but cannot afford one, or if he owns one but of inferior quality, or if he is the proud owner of a superb sword, and a higher-ranking noble covets it.

Weapons training, too, was available only to the upper classes. The lower classes did not have the time to devote to training.

In periods when life expectancy was far lower than it is today, when few children survived to adulthood, and when war, childbirth and disease killed most adults before they were forty, people had different attitudes to death. Your historical characters will probably be less shaken by a friend's death than a 21st century person, and they will have fewer qualms about killing.

In most periods and societies, women did not fight, so if you want your heroine to wield a weapon and kick butt, you need to find creative reasons why she is an exception. More about this in Chapter 15.

YOUNG ADULT

YA fight scenes are entertaining. Although they may involve violence, it is best to avoid gore. However, they may be very scary, especially in the Suspense section.

The plot often revolves around the protagonist performing implausible feats of fighting. To make those feats more plausible, give your protagonist martial arts skills. Perhaps she is the judo champion of her school, or a sub-plot focuses on her ambition to win a karate trophy, or maybe she is the star of the local capoeira performance team. See Chapter 11 and 13.

Choose a fight form about which you are knowledgeable, or whatever martial art teenagers currently consider to be cool.

CHILDREN'S FICTION

Fight scenes for children are pure entertainment. Pirates swashbuckle without spilling a drop of blood, and martial artists perform stunning acrobatics without strains or sprains. Take care, however, that you don't glorify violence. The scenes are usually short.

LITERARY

Either the fight takes place off-stage - so you don't write a fight scene at all - or it is shown in all its realistic brutality. Literary fight scenes are gritty. The fight itself is very short, and the Aftermath section is prolonged. The focus is on character development.

CHAPTER 27: CREATING EROTIC TENSION

Real fighting is seldom sexy - but in your story, you can make it sizzle. Here are some ideas.

Fight scenes and sex scenes have a lot in common, such as physical involvement, strong emotions, and the intense use of the senses.

HAND-TO-HAND FIGHTING

If at all possible, make it unarmed combat (hand-to-hand fight). In a one-to-one fight, the opponents have great physical awareness of each other and are totally focused on the other person's body and moves. You can use this to encompass erotic awareness.

The physical proximity and close touch, especially in grappling-type fight styles (e.g. wrestling), are similar to love-making, and rolling around on the mat in a tight clinch with a desirable person can be highly arousing.

If you're writing erotica, you add a touch of BDSM by using the power play: underlying sub/Dom (submissive/dominant - insiders capitalise 'Dom') desires can come to the fore, especially while pinning or getting pinned. Wrestling holds also offer scope for experiences which are deliciously painful yet safe.

DAGGERS

Armed fights have less potential for erotic tension, because weapons create not only a physical distance between the opponents, but an emotional one as well.

If you want to use a weapon, I recommend daggers. They are intimate and personal, with erotic connotations, and they often rouse intense emotions.

To stab someone with a dagger, the fighter has to get close, which makes it one of the most intimate weapons. When the dagger penetrates the flesh, the hand almost touches the victim. This is very different from a bullet or arrow, which can be shot from a great distance. The closeness creates an intensely personal connection between attacker and victim.

The shape of the weapon and the fact that it's typically worn on the belt make it a symbol of male virility. In many cultures and periods, men demonstrated their manhood by displaying ornate daggers at the front of their hips - the bigger, the better - and the hilt can be suggestively shaped. More about this in Chapter 5.

In addition, the motion of sliding a dagger into or out of the sheath can be highly suggestive. Talk about daggers lends itself to suggestive dialogue, with comments like

'Nice weapon. Are you any good at wielding it?', 'Want to see my other dagger, babe?', 'Does your dagger need polishing?', 'So you like swordplay, Milady? How about daggerplay?'

Book cover designers love daggers, especially when depicting the hero. They adore the chance to imply male virility. The elongated weapon on the hero's belt - or in the heroine's hand - hints at other things.

A dagger on the cover may increase your book's sex appeal, so it's worth telling your cover designer about it. However, many cover artists get carried away by the concept, with cringe-worthy results. I've seen covers where the hero wore the naked blade in his belt without a sheath: a prelude to self-mutilation!

MALE FANTASIES OF FEMALE FIGHTERS

Many men get turned on by watching females fight. If your heroine is a martial artist, and your hero has a fetish for warrior women, instant erotic tension ensues.

There are clubs where men pay to see women fight one another. Female/female fights are called 'catfights'. They involve wrestling, boxing, hair-pulling, and more.

Most of the time, these fights are choreographed shows, and the women receive a fixed fee per performance. Alternatively, they are competitive, only the winner who defeats all others gets paid, and the prize money is substantial. This leads to more realistic fighting, often ferocious and brutal.

Typically, the performers are healthy attractive young women who need money: college students, single mothers - perhaps the heroine of your novel?

A nastier version of these clubs involves women forced to fight: abducted girls, victims of human trafficking. The audience consist of men who enjoy seeing a woman's fear and pain. Such clubs are of course illegal, but they exist. They can be material for a thriller: perhaps the villain forces the heroine into fighting in order to punish her for defying him, or maybe she's seeking to rescue her younger sister, or she's an undercover cop infiltrating such a club.

Other men have fantasies about fighting the women, rather than watching them fight. If they're lucky, their wife has the same fancy, and they can indulge in gentle wrestling happily ever after. But far fewer women like wrestling men than the other way round. Consequently, men pay women to wrestle them.

These sessions often take place at an agency or 'wrestling studio' which employs part-time female wrestlers (attractive young women with some wrestling skill). When booking a session, the client chooses which girl he wants to wrestle, and pays per hour. It's not unlike sexual services - but there's nothing sexual going on (except in the man's mind and in his boxers). Woman and man both fight fully clothed. A staff member oversees the match acting as referee and chaperone to ensure the client doesn't take liberties.

The client gets a thrill from measuring his strength and skill against a woman's. Surprisingly, most of those men want to lose the match. Being defeated by a female and submitting to her is the pinnacle of their fantasies. Many clients are successful, powerful men at work - and in their private lives, they long to occasionally submit to a woman. Men with submissive wrestling fantasies are typically gentlemanly, courteous and considerate, which makes them suitable hero material.

WOMEN WATCHING MEN FIGHT

Alternatively, you can show men fighting, and describe the fight from an appreciative woman's (or gay man's) PoV. If the men wear sleeveless vests or fight with bare upper bodies, this gives you the opportunity to describe the play of muscles in back, arms and shoulders, as well as the sweat forming on the skin and other details. However, if the PoV is a woman watching her husband or lover fight, her experience will be more emotional than physical because she's concerned for his safety.

POST-FIGHT HORNINESS

Genuine fights aren't erotic - but they can build up an intense sexual charge.

Many law enforcement officers, women as well as men, find that after a dangerous fight, they get seriously horny. This is probably caused by the hormones which get injected into the bloodstream, combined with stress and the instinct to procreate when one's life is threatened. Most law enforcement officers have found ways of dealing with this sexual arousal. But in your story, you can use it to further the plot. Perhaps your heroine is a cop who faced an intense fight at the end of her workday - and she has a hot date that night. Or perhaps she and her male partner, after successfully overpowering the bad guys together, suddenly become aware of an attraction which hadn't been there before.

Although not all fighters experience sexual arousal after a fight, your heroine and hero certainly may.

CHAPTER 28: THE FINAL SHOWDOWN

Does your novel climax with a big showdown between the hero (or heroine) and the villain? Here are techniques to make this fight powerful and memorable.

* The fight scene during the novel's climax is longer than the other fight scenes in the book.

* It arouses the reader's emotions. Stir up as several layers of emotion - fear, hope, terror, love, loyalty, gratitude, despair - and make them intense.

* The climactic fight is often to the death. Either the hero or the villain must die, and they both know it. This makes their fight desperate.

* Raise the stakes as high as you can. In addition to the hero's life, something big is at stake, something he's prepared to die for: the freedom of the slaves, the life of his lover, the safety of the orphans, the future of Earth.

* The fight at the climax represents the fight for the protagonist's cause. What is the big cause the hero has been pursuing throughout the novel? Put this at stake, and the reader will sit on the edge of her chair.

* State the purpose of the fight, that big cause for which the hero is fighting. Spell it out, and keep it in the reader's mind. The more you emphasise the purpose, the more the readers will root for the hero.

* Use an unusual location for the fight, preferably a dangerous place, such as burning house, a narrow rope-bridge across a ravine, or a sinking ship.

* Stack the odds against your hero by giving the villain the better weapons, better armour, better preparation. Make your hero vulnerable: he's unarmed or poorly armed, without protective armour, maybe even injured or exhausted. The more you stack the odds, the more the readers will root for the hero. While this applies to all fight scenes, it's especially important at the Climax. Make it almost impossible for the hero to win.

* If several people are involved in the fight, arrange it so there are more bad guys than good guys, because readers always root for the minority.

* If the villain is supported by several henchmen, let your hero defeat them one by one. The villain has to be the last one to fall, in order to keep the tension high.

* Show violence. Even if you've skirted around violence in the earlier parts of the novel, this scene will benefit from injury and pain.

* Create a 'black moment' when all seems lost. Then the hero recalls his purpose, rallies his last drop of strength and courage, and fights on until victory.

* If your hero has a special skill, find a way to use it in the fight scene, preferably in a surprising way.

* If your hero has a weakness, phobia or fear, force him to face it during the climactic fight. For example, if he fears heights, the fight takes place on the roof of a skyscraper. If he has a phobia of snakes, the villain uses snakes against him. If he's terrified of spiders, he must fight in a spider-infested cave.

BLUNDERS TO AVOID

* Making it easy for the hero ... as if he couldn't rise to a genuine challenge

* Not enough is at stake
* The climactic fight is so brief that the reader almost misses it

CHAPTER 29: PACING

Fight scenes need a fast pace – perhaps faster than any other scene in the novel. How do you achieve a really fast pace?

First, put on some fast music while you write. For suggestions, see Chapter 32.

The pace is probably fastest in the Start, Action, Surprise and Climax sections. In the Suspense and Aftermath sections the pace is usually slow.

Here are some technical tricks for manipulating the pace.

TRICKS FOR FAST PACE

1. Short words

Words with a single syllable are best. Avoid words with more than three syllables. For example: Instead of 'immediately' write 'at once'. Instead of 'endeavour' write 'try'. Instead of 'indicate' write 'point at'. Instead of 'investigate' write 'check out'.

2. Short sentences

The shorter, the better. If a sentence is more than twelve words long, split it into two shorter ones. Avoid sentences with many clauses. Some sentences can be very short indeed:

He leaped.

She kicked.

Blades clanked.

To vary the rhythm, insert the occasional medium-length sentence, but avoid long ones.

3. Partial sentences

When the action is at its fastest, you can use sentence fragments. For example:

He had to get through to the castle. Had to reach that door. He hacked, swung, slashed. Five paces left. He leaped.

Use this trick sparingly, only for the fastest-paced moments, since it becomes tedious if overused.

4. Short paragraphs

Keep the paragraphs shorter than average in your book. Some sentences may be a single line. If a paragraph is longer than four lines, split it up.

5. Lots of verbs

Verbs convey action and create a fast pace. You can use several verbs in a sentence, for example:

She bit, she scratched, she screamed.

They slashed and sliced, they blocked and parried.

To make it easy for you, I've compiled a list of verbs for fight scenes. Simply pick the ones which suit your kind of fighting and fill your scene with them.

act, alter, attack, avert, back, bang, bash, battle, beat, beg, belt, bend, best, bite, blacken, bleed, blind, blister, block, blow, blunt, boil, bolt, boot, bore, bow, box, brace, brag, brash, brawl, break, breathe, brush, buck, bulge, burn, burst, cackle, call, can, carry, cart, carve, catch, check, chop, chuck, clack, clank, clap, clash, claw, clear, cleave, click, cliff, cling, clink, clip, close, club, cock, coil, cold, collar, come, con, connect, corner, cost, count, counter, cover, cower, crack, crackle, cram, crash, crawl, creep, crinkle, cross, crouch, crush, cry, cuff, cull, cup, curl, curse, curve, cusp, cut, dart, dash, deepen, dig, deep, dip, ditch, drive, drop, duck, dump, edge, effect, erect, escape, exert, expect, feint, fight, fire, fist, fit, flag, flare, flash, flick, fling, flip, flock, force, gash, gasp, get, gore, grab, grasp, grip, grope, group, hack, harden, heat, help, hit, hop, hurl, hurry, impale, jab, jar, jerk, join, jolt, jump, keep, kick, kill, knee, knock, knot, knuckle, leak, leap, let, lever, lick, lift, lock, loop, lop, plunge, mask, nick, nip, open, oppose, pace, pack, pain, pair, pale, palm, pan, pant, parry, part, pass, paste, pat, peak, peck, pelt, pick, pierce, pile, ping, piss, pit, pivot, plot, pluck, plug, plunge, ply, point, pool, pop, pose, pot, pound, pour, powder, pray, preen, prepare, prey, prick, prickle, print, probe, pry, pull, pulp, pulse, pump, punch, pursue, push, quarry, quarter, quest, race, raise, rake, ram, rap, rasp, rear, retreat, rip, riposte, rivet, roar, rock, roll, rope, round, rouse, run, rush, sap, scale, scalp, scan, score, scream, seek, seep, shake, shape, sharpen, shock, shoot, shop, slam, slap, slash, slice, slick, slip, slit, smash, snap, snare, snatch, snipe, sock, space, spar, spark, speed, spike, spill, spin, spit, splash, spoil, spring, spur, spurt, spy, squirm, stand, start, steer, step, stick, strap, strike, stuff, suck, support, swat, sweat, sweep, swing, swish, tack, tag, taint, take, target, taste, team, tear, tent, test, thrash, throw, thrust thud, thwart, tick, tide, tilt, time, tire, top, toss, tower, toy, trap, trick, trigger, trip, triumph, trouble, trump, try, tuck, tug, turn, twirl, twitch, weaken, wet, whip, whirl, whirr, whoop, whoosh, whop, work, zap, zip

(Note: Although many words in this list are nouns as well as verbs, use them as verbs where possible.)

6. Few adjectives and adverbs

Use adjectives (blunt, strong, irresistible) sparingly, and avoid adverbs (bluntly, strongly, irresistibly) altogether.

7. Tenses

Simple Past Tense (hacked, swung, slashed, kicked) is the best for fast-paced action. Avoid Past Perfect Tense (had hacked, had swung, had slashed, had kicked) because it's a pace-killer.

Be careful about using the ing-form of the verb (present participles and gerunds: hacking, swinging, slashing, kicking). Although it conveys immediacy, it sounds soft and can spoil the pace, so use it sparingly.

8. Avoid link words

Use as few conjunctions and link words (and, but, or, when, then, after, before, while, because, in order to, therefore, thereby, as) as possible. For example, instead of

He grabbed the liana with both hands, and then he swung across the stream and landed in the mud.

write

He grabbed the liana with both hands, swung across the stream, landed in the mud.

Instead of:

After that, he raised his arm, thereby warding off blows.

write

He raised his arm to ward off blows.

9. Avoid internal thoughts

Don't allow your protagonist to think, consider, wonder, analyse, realise, worry or contemplate during the fight. During the Suspense and the Aftermath, he may think as much as he wants, but not in the other sections. Any kind of introspection slows the pace.

If it's absolutely necessary to render his thoughts, do it as briefly as possible. Here are three examples:

Now.

He had to win.

Where was the cavalry?

TRICKS FOR SLOW PACE

For the Suspense and Aftermath sections of your scene, consider slowing the pace. This will create a fantastic contrast to the fast-paced action of the fight.

1. Use medium-length and long sentences

2. The paragraphs are longer: three lines minimum.

3. Include some words of three or more syllables.

4. Use some adjectives and maybe a couple of adverbs.

5. Insert thoughts. Let us look inside the PoV's head as he assesses the terrain, plans a strategy, or mourns his friend.

BLUNDERS TO AVOID

* The hero has deep and meaningful thoughts during combat... as if he the fighting did not require his full attention

* The hero considers the consequences of every movement carefully before he strikes... as if he had time for that

* Detailed descriptions once the fighting has started... as if the PoV had time to admire the scenery and his opponent's fashion sense

* Lengthy, convoluted sentences ... as if fighting was a leisurely, slow-paced activity

* Lots of adverbs... as if any sense of speed created by a verb must be squashed instantly

CHAPTER 30: EUPHONICS

Certain sounds have certain effects on the psyche. By using words which include those sounds, you influence how the reader feels. This is a subtle trick for manipulating the reader's subconscious.

FOREBODING

To create a sense of worry, unease, doom and foreboding, use words with 'ow', 'oh', 'ou', 'oo' sounds. These are perfect for the Suspense section, when the hero readies himself for a fight he would rather avoid, or when the heroine senses danger but does not yet know where the threat is coming from. Try: moor, growl, slow, wound, soon, doom, show, grow, tow, loom, howl, mound, cower.

SPOOKY

Use words with 's' sounds, if possible combined with short 'i' sounds: hiss, sizzle, crisp, sister, whisper, sinister, glisten, stick. These can work well in the Suspense section of a thriller or urban fantasy.

ACUTE FEAR

To convey the PoV's acute fear, use words with 'ee/ea' sounds, if possible combine with a few 's' sounds. These are perfect to use when the PoV is scared, perhaps in the Suspense section, in the Climax when he thinks he's about to be killed, or when the stone bridge has collapsed and the fight moves onto a narrow frayed rope bridge across a deep chasm. Try: squeal, scream, stream, squeeze, creak, steal, fear, clear, sheer.

FIGHTING ACTION

Once the fighting is on - especially if it involves fists, swords or daggers - use short words with 't', 'p' and 'k' sounds. They are great for the Start, Action and Climax sections. Try: *cut, block, top, shoot, tackle, trick, kick, crack, grip, grab, grope, punch, drop, pound, poke, cop, chop.*

SPEED

Short words containing 'r' speed up the pace - ideal for the Start, Action and Climax sections. Try: *run, race, riot, rage, red, roll, rip, hurry, thrust, scurry, ring, crack.*

TROUBLE

Words containing 'tr' signal trouble, problems and plot complications. Depending on the story, they may well serve well in the Suspense, Surprise and Climax sections. Try: *trouble, trap, trip, trough, treat, trick, treasure, atrocious, attract, petrol, trance, try, traitor.*

MACHO POWER

If you want to emphasise the fighters' masculinity or authority, use 'p' sounds. They plant ideas of power, law enforcement, and maleness into the reader's mind. Try: *pole, power, police, cop, pile, pry, prong, post, pillar, push, pass, punch, crop, crop, crap, trap, pack, point, part* (as well as a number of names for male genitals).

PUNISHMENT

If your fight scene involves punishment or erotic dominance, consider using words with 'str'. Try: *strict, strive, astride, strike, stripe, stray, strong, strident, stroke, strip, instruct, castrate.*

DEFEAT

Use 'd' sounds to convey a sense of dejection and despair. Try: *drop, dead, deep, dark, dull, depressed, despair, dump, dig, down, dank, damp, darkness, drag, ditch.*

VICTORY

'J' and 'ch' sounds serve best to create a triumphant happy mood. Try: *joy, cheer, jubilant, jeer, chuck, chariot, choose, chip, joke, jest, jamboree, jig, jazz, jive, rejoice, rejoin.*

PERFORMANCE

Euphonics are especially powerful when the reader actually hears the words. If you're writing a story for radio, are planning to publish your novel as an audiobook, or intend to give author readings at your local book shop, euphonics help enthral your audience.

DISADVANTAGES

In print, the effects of this technique are very subtle, serving only to enhance what's already there. It needs to be combined with other techniques.

If you use too many similar-sounding words close together, the effect can be comical rather than scary.

Using words which have the right sound but the wrong meaning weakens your scene. Use euphonics only when there's a choice of suitable words.

CHAPTER 31: SABRE-SHARP DIALOGUE

Dialogue in a fight scene can be either entertaining, or it can be realistic. It can't be both.

Your choice in Chapter 1 - 'entertaining' or 'gritty' - decides what kind of dialogue your fight scene contains.

In an entertaining scene, there's a lot of verbal sparring. The fighters trade zingers at the same time as sword blows. Readers love those witty repartees. Make every single line of dialogue a zinger, and cut any word that doesn't advance the plot or entertain the reader.

In a gritty scene, opponents don't talk while they're fighting. Dialogue is implausible in a real fight. Panting with effort, the fighters don't have breath to spare for verbal banter. Focused on different action every fraction of a second, dodging sword blows, trying to get their own hits in, they aren't able to compose articulate statements, let alone think of profound observations and witty repartees.

Any dialogue in the gritty scene has to happen before the fight starts, in the Suspense section. The survivor may say something profound in the Aftermath.

If your fight scene is 'entertaining with gritty elements' - typical for romance novels - then you need to make the dialogue seem plausible even if it isn't. Create an illusion of reality by using very short dialogue sentences.

TRICKS FOR SABRE-SHARP DIALOGUE

1. Put most of the verbal sparring into the Suspense section. During the 'Start of the Fight', they may use taunts to provoke the other into rash actions. During the other sections, they don't talk, unless there's a pause in the fighting.

2. In the Aftermath, the winner delivers a parting phrase which can be profound or funny (or both).

3. Use short, even incomplete, sentences to convey the out-of-breath state.

Implausible dialogue during a sword fight:

"Now that you've had a taste of my sword, will you give up and surrender to my superior strength?"

"Never in my life will I surrender to one as evil as you. Do to me what you will, but I will not submit."

"Then you must take the consequences of your choice."

Plausible version:

"Give up?"

"Never."

"Then take this!"

4. Don't write "Ugh", "Argh", "Ouch". Those look fine in graphic novels and comic books, but silly in novels.

5. Give one or both fighters a catchphrase. This is a sentence the character speaks several times in the novel, in different contexts. Readers love it when the catchphrase comes up in the fight scene.

For example: the heroine works in a fashion boutique, and asks a tedious customer "How do you like this one?" When choosing which puppy to adopt from the shelter, she asks her boyfriend, "How do you like this one?" In the fight scene, she slashes the villain's cheek with her rapier, and asks "How do you like this one?"

A bizarre catchphrase such as "Man, you need a haircut," can become really funny in a fight scene where the speaker wields a slashing sword.

Catchphrases are fun and memorable. You may remember some from books you've read and films you've watched.

Examples: "I'll be back" (*The Terminator*), "Hasta la vista, baby" (*The Terminator 2*), "Make my day" (*Sudden Impact*), "Resistance is futile" (*Star Trek*), "Hello, my name is Inigo Montoya, you killed my father, prepare to die." (*The Princess Bride*).

FAMOUS EXAMPLES

Here are some famous film fight scenes, worth watching to see how their dialogue is handled:

Sanjuro: An excellent example of a gritty fight scene in which the dialogue happens during the Suspense section and the survivor delivers a statement at the Aftermath. (For copyright reasons, this clip is short and does not include the Suspense and Aftermath sections. Watch the movie if you get the chance.)

http://www.youtube.com/watch?v=3YQcpcNsEtg

The Princess Bride - Inigo Montoya vs the Man in Black. A fun entertaining fight scene, famous for its dialogue zingers. Highly implausible, but delightful. Almost every sentence is witty and memorable.
http://www.youtube.com/watch?v=8-66KBi_NM0

The Princess Bride: Inigo Montoya vs Count Rugen. An entertaining fight scene with some gritty elements. Observe the repetition of the famous catchphrase.

http://www.youtube.com/watch?v=d6m7NR6iYjg

BLUNDERS TO AVOID

* Fighters holding a leisurely conversation with long, carefully articulated sentences... as if they had plenty of breath to spare during the swashbuckling

CHAPTER 32: BACKGROUND MUSIC

While writing your fight scene, play music in the background. The tempo of the music will affect your heart rate as well as your subconscious. Fast, bouncy music leads to fast-paced scenes, while ambient relaxation music can give your scene the pace of a slug.

Ideally, the music you play in the background should have medium or fast tempo. It helps if it's instrumental, because lyrics can distract from writing. Perhaps you can even find tunes which suit the mood, culture, period or setting of your story.

Consider burning a CD or creating a playlist for your fight scene writing sessions.

Here are some of the tunes I play while writing fight scenes. At YouTube, you can listen to them for free - just don't be tempted to watch the clips when you should be writing.

* *Sabre Dance* by Aram Khachaturian. Very fast, exciting, perfect for sword or dagger fights.

http://www.youtube.com/watch?v=gqg3l3r_DRI

* The final of the overture to the opera *William Tell* (aka *Wilhelm Tell* aka *Guillaume Tell*) by Giaochino Rossini. Very fast, great for cavalry charges.

http://www.youtube.com/watch?v=xoHECVnQC7A

* *Ceddin Denden*, a traditional Turkish military song. Medium tempo, good for historical fiction.

http://www.youtube.com/watch?v=ntVtN3g6ERM

* *Walkürenritt* aka *Ride of the Valkyries* by Richard Wagner. Dramatic and intense, good for final showdown fights at the climax of the novel.

http://www.youtube.com/watch?v=V92OBNsQgxU

* *Unstoppable* by E.S. Posthumus. Dramatic, good for gritty scenes.

http://www.youtube.com/watch?v=VoaUYcwEpSw

* *Kafkas Lezginka* (aka *Kavkas Lezginka*), a traditional tune from the Caucasus, used for ultra-masculine folk dance performances. Good for dagger and fencing fights.

http://www.youtube.com/watch?v=3eqt6mPenUM&feature=related

* *Seyh Samil* aka *Sheik Shamil* aka *Seyx Schamil* and various other spellings. A famous folk song from the Caucasus and the Middle East, celebrating the heroism of a historical resistance leader. This is an instrumental version with a steady rhythm.

http://www.youtube.com/watch?v=_-Qzp2yw8xw

You can also listen to military marches, which generally have a steady medium-to-fast rhythm. However, their exuberant mood, designed to make soldiers happy about going to war, may not be ideal unless you're writing an entertaining scene.

Movie soundtracks, especially from fight scenes, are often dramatic and intense and can help you get in the mood. Unfortunately, they often lack the steady rhythm most authors need for writing.

CHAPTER 33: RESEARCH

Further research is fun and can give your scenes greater authenticity.

It's worth finding out more about your hero's weapon, especially if you're working on a series of novels, or focussing on a period. For example, if you write medieval romances, research medieval weapons, armour, tournaments and battle strategies, and if you write samurai stories, get a thorough understanding of katana swords.

Instead of spending years on becoming an expert, spend an hour talking to someone who is an expert already. Experts love talking about their subject, especially to writers.

Browse Yahoo Groups, Google Communities and other online social networks for groups of sword enthusiasts, gun enthusiasts, archery enthusiasts, anything enthusiasts. Here are two groups worth joining:

Rayne's Writers Research Club. This Yahoo Group devoted to helping writers with research. It's open to all writers at all levels. This is where you can ask what a shotgun sounds like and whether the blood from a slashed abdomen seeps or spurts, as well as more gentle things like what dawn smells like on the banks of the Nile or how a five-year old talks.

Membership is free. All we ask is that you contribute answers when someone asks about your subjects of expertise. (Sooner or later, someone will ask something you can answer from experience, e.g. something to do with your job, your hobby, your pets, or the place where you live). Please ask lots of questions. We love people who ask questions. **groups.yahoo.com/group/raynes_writers_research/**

Weapons Info. This is a Yahoo online group especially for writers who have questions, and for weapons experts who like to show off their knowledge. They experts seem to have detailed knowledge especially about guns. They can tell you what kind of gun your heroine can hide in her bra and what kind of wound which kind of gun causes at which distance.
groups.yahoo.com/group/Weapons_Info/

You can also contact historical re-enactment societies in your area, or your local branch of the Society for Creative Anachronism.

YouTube has lots of clips of weapons demonstrations and re-enactments, of varying quality. Once you've chosen your weapon, you can probably find many YouTube clips about it. For demonstrations of different types of swords, I value the ones by Cold Steel, a manufacturer of replica weapons. For medieval weapons and armour, I like the documentaries presented by Peter Woodward.

YouTube also offers many martial arts displays. Once you've chosen the kind of fighting you want to use, type the name of a martial art (e.g. aikido, karate, boxing) into the YouTube browser, and you'll get a whole list of clips where competent instructors demonstrate manoeuvres. Pick a series of manoeuvres and model your fight on them. This guarantees a plausible fight. You can replay the clip as often as you need to get it right. (Caution: using 'wrestling' as a search word brings up a lot of 'adult' entertainment).

When looking for self-defence demonstrations, try both the British and the American spelling ('self- defence' and 'self-defense'). You'll find some great moves your heroine can use to get out of tricky situations. Beware, though: some of the coolest-looking manoeuvres work only on a very obliging attacker. The demonstrations by Tony Agostini strike me as ingenious as well as practical.

You may want to watch history documentaries television or hire DVDs; most of those show correct weaponry and fighting techniques.

Movie fight scenes are better for inspiration and for studying dramatic structure than for research.

Major films produced in the past twenty years are usually historically accurate and carefully researched, but older films often contain amazing blunders. Older Hollywood films (especially those starring Errol Flynn) dazzle more with their choreography than their historical accuracy. Fighters use weapons and techniques which were not invented until centuries later.

The worldwide web is full of articles about weapons, written by experts (or wannabe experts). It's worth checking the author's credentials. Broadly speaking, the websites of large re-enactment societies and historical research organisations contain the best material.

I also recommend browsing the online catalogues of replica weapons manufacturers; these give clear pictures and brief explanations. Avoid the ones devoted to 'fantasy weapons' and any weapons with fancy names like 'Saladin's Magic Scimitar' and 'Queen Cleopatra's Dagger of Doom'.

And, of course, there are books on every kind of weapon, varying in tone from sensational to the academic. For the bluffer, illustrated children's books are a wonderful source, because they provide easy-to-understand explanations.

Consider finding out about less well-known weapons. How about a bardiche (polearm), a war hammer, an urumi (whip sword), a nunchaku, a flail, a kerambit (claw dagger), a morgenstern (spiked mace), a hunga munga (spiked throwing blade)? These will make your fight scene stand out from the usual stuff, and rouse the interest of jaded readers.

If your book contains several fight scenes, varying the weapons makes it interesting. Even if your hero always fights with his trusted sword, the evil overlord can wield an urumi, the rebel a chakram and the villainous henchmen in the army of doom can use morgensterns.

You can have fun browsing the web for interesting weapons. Suggested starting sites:

http://medieval.stormthecastle.com/essays/unusual-medieval-weapons.htm (unusual medieval weapons)

http://www.weirdasianews.com/2007/08/31/weird-asian-martial-arts-weapons/ (Asian martial arts weapons)

http://youtu.be/sDNw2slOK3Y (the Sikh chakram throwing disk)

If you are aiming to give your fight scenes realism, I recommend the e-book *Violence - A Writers' Guide*. It is filled with insights and practical information about the psychology of violence, and can help you with the characterisation of the fighters as well as with the plotting of the scene. The author has plenty of experience and expertise in the subject, and he writes well.

Another book you may find useful is *Them's Fightin' Words! A Writer's Guide For Writing Fight Scenes* by Teel James Glenn. It may help especially with choreographing entertaining sword fight scenes. However, it seems to be currently out of print.

Write the Fight Right by Alan Baxter is a recently published book, short, well-written and readable.

Learning to do it yourself will give you a feel for what it's like and help avoid blunders. You can sign up for classes or workshops in your hero's fighting skill. However, this is a time-consuming research method, and bear in mind that your hero's advanced perspective will differ from your beginner-level experience.

CHAPTER 34: EXCERPTS

FIGHT SCENE EXCERPT FROM *STORM DANCER*

Here's an excerpt from my dark heroic novel *Storm Dancer*, midway between gritty and entertaining. I've applied many of the techniques covered in this book – see if you can spot them.

Dahoud was stiff and dizzy from days on the rack. Flexing his back against the tent pole, he fought for balance. Tentative stretches opened his scabbed wounds, sending dribbles of blood down his legs.

[...]

As soon as the soldier had left, Dahoud picked up the sword Merida had dropped and tested it in his hand. The grip fit comfortably in his palm and the weight of the curved blade was familiar, a sister to his own sword.

He scanned the tent. With the anchored torture table in the centre, the big chair on one side and the brazier on the other, Baryush would have no room for elaborate manoeuvres.

He dropped the turban and dagger and kicked off Kirral's tight shoes. Bare soles gave a better hold on the slippery straw. With his sword in his right, and the bucket in place of a shield, he took position beside the tent entrance.

With luck, Baryush would take the message to mean his enemy was free and waiting. With luck, he would rush into the tent alone. With luck, he would take a moment to see the naked captive tied to the table was Kirral, giving Dahoud time to strike. With luck, Baryush was an unskilled swordsman. With luck, a single quick slash to the throat would suffice.

Dahoud would need a lot of luck.

[…] Bending his legs into a fighting stance, he listened for sounds from the outside. Horses whinnied, armour clanked, soldiers cursed.

Dahoud waited. And waited. The scabbed wounds itched, and more blood oozed.

[…]

Standing in fighting stance stretched the wounded flesh of Dahoud's thighs. Blood trickled down his legs.

At last, the entrance flap thudded and Baryush stormed in, his jewels flashing, the hem of his robe brushing the straw, his sword naked and ready to strike. Alone.

At the sight of the tied captive, he halted only for a heartbeat. Then he spun to block Dahoud's slash. Bronze clanked on bronze.

Dahoud struck again. Once more, his blow glanced off Baryush's blade. Baryush slashed downwards, past the bucket-shield, at Dahoud's leg. Dahoud jumped back just in time so the sword only grazed his skin.

Dahoud shoved the bucket against his opponent, sending him back in a stagger. For an instant, Baryush fought for balance, and his sandals slipped on the straw. Dahoud aimed for the throat, but Baryush evaded. The blade cut only his arm. Baryush swung his sword faster than Dahoud could anticipate. This time, the sword sliced deeper into the side of his thigh.

"Thank you for the invitation." Baryush spoke with effortless courtesy, as if the line of crimson beading on his arm was nothing, as if the fighting did not even speed his breath. His eyes glinted like obsidian flakes. "I trust Kirral will tell me how you got free. The chance to kill you gilds my day."

Weakened from deprivation and blood loss, Dahoud's limbs threatened to fold.

Baryush lunged, and blade crashed against blade. The Darrian was strong, fast, and fit. Even his long robe barely hampered his agility.

[...]

Blood ran down Dahoud's cheeks, although he did not recall cuts to his face. More blood was seeping from his thigh, and his strength with it.

"Tired, Besieger?"

Dahoud tried every trick of swordcraft he knew, made every attempt the limited space permitted, threw every drop of skill into the fight, but could not match the blinding speed of Baryush's blade. He barely managed to block the attacks. The sword grip in his palm was slick with sweat and blood.

He must keep the sword moving, must maintain the fluid curves, must not halt the flow, or Baryush would break through. The Mare Mother be thanked, he still had strength in his sword arm, even as his knees started to buckle. On horseback, he had always swung his sword in a figure-eight. But there was no room for wide arcs in the tent.

"Were you hoping for a quick death? There will be nothing fast," Baryush promised. "Not for the Besieger." His blade hissed through the air. "I'll have the pleasure of slicing you limb by limb. Your life will bleed into the straw."

The air was thick with the smells of Baryush's cedarwood perfume, charcoal smoke and sweat. Dahoud's pulse pounded as if about to burst his chest, his bones jolted with every blow, and dizziness draped around him like a strangling mist.

His vision blurred. All he could still see clearly was the flames of the oil lamps reflected in Baryush's jewels, in his eyes, in his sword.

Blood dripped from his forehead into his eyes, blinding him. He backed away from the force of the general's fury until the edge of the torture table pressed into his back. A hard strike knocked the sword from his grip. It clattered to the ground. Now he held but a wooden bucket against the pelting blows.

Baryush would aim for Dahoud's knee, and the next stroke would cripple him. Had he lost his chance to kill Baryush and save Koskara? Merida was counting on him.

[...]

The table was almost as high as a horse. No time or space for a run. He shoved the bucket in Baryush's face, threw his hands back to brace against the table edge, and took his body weight on both arms. He chambered both legs and snapped them forward, slamming them against Baryush's thighs. While Baryush stumbled, Dahoud raised himself up on his arms again. This time, he pushed himself forward, his legs wide.

He crashed against his opponent, landed on top of him.

The impact knocked the brazier. Sparks showered and charcoal scattered. Rustling flames rose and crept under the table, gnawing at the damp straw. The air stunk of Kirral's piss and smouldering felt. Scratchy smoke thickened the air.

Dahoud pinned Baryush and tried to prise the sword from his hand. He was the better wrestler, but his body was stiff and weakened from wounds. His thighs barely had the strength to hold Baryush underneath him.

Then the straw burst into orange. The heat bit into Dahoud's seared thighs.

Panting, they fought for possession of the weapon. Baryush tossed it to the tent flap, where Dahoud could not reach it without releasing his hold.

Kirral's curved dagger lay in the burning straw. Dahoud used all the strength of his right arm to keep Baryush's wrists pinned to the ground, and stretched towards the weapon. Flames gnawed at his hand as he snatched the dagger from the burning straw.

"One last time, Baryush: I'm sorry for what I did to your sister. But I'm not sorry for killing you."

He drew the blade across Baryush's throat. Blood shot up and showered him in its hot spurt.

Dahoud stood, knife in hand, and slammed a salute for his dead enemy.

[...]

Trembling with fatigue, Dahoud kicked the smouldering straw away from the table. […] He had to help Mansour's army to win the battle.

[This leads directly into another fight scene, hence no Aftermath.]

FIGHT SCENE EXCERPT FROM *SCYLLA AND THE PEPPER PIRATES*

This is a brief scene from my humorous fantasy short story *Scylla and the Pepper Pirates* published in *Cutlass: Ten Tales of Pirates*. This fight is entertaining without gritty elements.

I strode across the gangplank, dumped my cloth-sack at his feet, and spoke through haughtily pursed lips. "Who is Foxhead's current mistress? Get her on deck."

Now I had his attention. His green eyes sparkled, and a tongue-tip flickered across his lips. "Will there be a fight?"

Leaning against a stack of crates, I twirled my long golden braid and tapped my foot.

"I'll get Mimibella at once. First Mate Hulbert at your service." He doffed his pointy cap and scurried down the hatch.

Moments later, a woman came flouncing out, hooped petticoats whipping, curves heaving like waves on a stormy sea.

"I'm the master's mistress," Mimibella squealed. "Get off my ship."

I pulled off my crimson gloves and tossed them at her velvet-slippered feet. "I invoke the Ancient Law of the Sea. If you want to keep your captain, get ready to fight."

I could already taste the honey sweetness of an easy victory: this puppet in frills and flounces was no fighter.

"Do something!" she demanded of the sailors who swarmed around our show like flies around a cow-pat. "You know me. I've sailed on the *Hippolyta* for eight months! Mr Hulbert, throw this bitch off! Boolibar, cast a spell on her!"

Hulbert dragged a coil of rope out of our way and rubbed his hands. The ship's wizard, a small black-skinned man whose chest gleamed with silver amulets, heaved himself onto a pork barrel to watch. The others glanced from my opponent to me, shuffled their bare feet and shrugged.

With leather boots, breeches and jerkin, I was more suitably dressed for the occasion than the floozy in her finery. While she fumed and stamped, I went into fighting stance, legs braced, knees bent, fists balled in front of my face.

Instead of trembling, she snapped her fingers. "Mr. Hulbert! Slice my laces!"

Lip-licking, he applied his dirk, and the corselet dropped to the planks. Her storm-wave breasts, no longer restricted by whale-boned brocade, bounced freely in her chemise. Another dozen sailors clustered around us, pretending to scrub the deck.

A quick fumble at her waist, the skirt clanked to the ground and Mimibella stood in her fetching frillies. Swiftly, she stepped out of her hoops and bent her legs into a fighter's crouch. "You daughter of a brain-dead bat want to take my captain?"

Before I could attack, her head rammed into my belly.

Gasping for air, I stumbled back. A right jab followed so fast I had no time to sidestep it. Her fists were steel hammers used to work. Maybe I should have chosen an easier target.

I got a good punch under her armpit that sent her howling. She responded by crashing a hammer fist on my head. A door slammed shut behind my eyes. All went dark. Then I saw sparkles.

The darkness cleared, and I remembered my purpose. I simply had to win my place on this ship, or my beloved would be lost.

I grasped her raven locks and yanked. "Piss-soup dumpling!"

She retaliated by grabbing my plait. "Stinking mother of a mule!"

I got in several good punches. Droplets of blood oozed from my knuckles. Her chemise clung, wet with sweat. We punched and pulled, cursed and kicked. She had the better curses. I had the better kicks.

With a kick to her buttocks, I sent her slithering across the planks. I grabbed her by the chemise, pulled her up, clamped one arm around her neck. Then I ran, yanking her with me, and rammed her head into the stacked crates. Once, twice. Once more. I heard the wood crash and let her limp body drop.

Not long after, she roused herself, groaned and counted her bruises. Her black eyes shot me a hateful stare. "You bitch born from a rotten snake egg!" she cursed as she limped off the ship, not even trying to retrieve her belongings from the cabin. "Spawn of a thousand harpies! Barnacle-crusted flax-wench! Clapper-clawed harbour rat!"

I wasn't worried about Mimibella's fate. With a chest like hers, displayed in battle-soiled frothies, she'd soon find another captain, even if the ship wasn't as fine as the *Hippolyta*.

With as much grace as my battered bones permitted, I strode aft to make myself at home in the captain's cabin.

Dear Reader,

I hope you've enjoyed this book and gained many practical ideas for your writing. If you found it helpful, I'll be thrilled if you post a review on Amazon, Barnes&Noble, GoodReads, or wherever you purchased it or are a member.

If you email me the URL to your review, I'll send you a review ebook of one of my other Writer's Craft books: *Writing Scary Scenes, Writing about Magic, The Word-Loss Diet, Writing About Villains, Writing About Magic, Writing Dark Stories, Writing Short Stories to Promote Your Novels, Twitter for Writers, Why Does My Book Not Sell? 20 Simple Fixes, Writing Vivid Settings.* Tell me which one you want, and I'll send you the ebook free.

Let me know if you've found any errors, omissions, broken links or typos in this book. Some errors always sneak past the eagle eyes of the proofreaders. Also contact me if you have questions. My email is **rayne_hall_author@yahoo.com**. I look forward to hearing from you.

Perhaps you know other writers who might benefit from this book? Tell them about it.

On Twitter, you can follow me @RayneHall. **http://twitter.com/RayneHall** I'm very active on Twitter; it's my preferred social network. If you tweet that you've read this book, I'll follow you back – though you may have to remind me, because I have many followers and it's easy to miss a tweet.

Sincere thanks to everyone who helped with this book, including the members of the Professional Authors group and Rayne's Writers Research Club, as well as the students who participated in my 'Writing Fight Scenes' workshops, asked stimulating questions, and made me think about their scenes. You know who you are.

Rayne Hall

CPSIA information can be obtained at www.ICGtesting.com
Printed in the USA
LVOW10s0527111016

507661LV00001B/41/P